LOST FOX CITIES

SCOTT WITTMAN

The History Press

Published by The History Press
Charleston, SC
www.historypress.com

Front cover: Consolidated Papers–Appleton Division, circa 1948. Erected in 1886 on the site of the second Richmond Mill, it was razed in 1984. *Courtesy of the Andrew J. Mueller Collection at the History Museum at the Castle. Back cover top:* Two employees posing in 1902 at Thilmany Mill. *Courtesy of the Paper Discovery Center. Back cover bottom:* Kimberly-Clark Kimberly Mill, circa 1910. Razed in 2011. *Courtesy of the Winnebago County Historical and Archaeological Society.*

First published 2019

Manufactured in the United States

ISBN 9781467140331

Library of Congress Control Number: 2018963662

To the purveyors of preservation: the small-town historical societies, researchers and local history museums who carry on, with little to no funding, recognition or credit, to save our stories...

CONTENTS

PROLOGUE

In the mid-1990s, barely out of my teens, I left the only home I'd ever known in Appleton, Wisconsin, and traveled west, fulfilling a need to explore the world outside of the Fox Cities. After all, I thought, nothing would ever change here. The Fox Cities were paper mill towns. I didn't know why or how that came to be, it just always was.

The Badger-Globe and Atlas Mills had been here for one-hundred-plus years and they certainly weren't going anywhere. I had friends whose fathers worked at Gilbert and Glatfelter, just like their grandfathers did, and generations to follow would too, of course. The Kimberly Mill, then called Repap, employed hundreds of people in Kimberly and Little Chute, and the world I saw here just never stopped turning. Therefore, I figured, the milling industry being not for me, I needed to cut my teeth elsewhere.

So off I went. To the Rockies of Colorado and Utah, the deserts of Nevada, the plains of the Dakotas and all the places in between. There, I learned my passions and immersed myself in the history of these lands, which were strange to me at the time. I researched the lives of the miners, the forty-niners, the homesteaders, the saloonkeepers, the immigrants, the Native Americans and those who manifested, for good and bad, the American Destiny.

It was also during this time that I came to the somewhat sobering realization that my knowledge of the history of the place that I came from was underwhelming, to say the least.

When I returned home for good in the early 2000s, the place I used to think would never change was in the beginning stages of a generational transformation the depths of which many still today struggle to bring to terms.

Both the Badger-Globe and Atlas Mills were gone, the former being wiped from the landscape and the latter morphing into a museum. Several years later, Gilbert and Glatfelter were consumed by the global market, vanquished from sight by wrecking balls. The Kimberly Mill followed within months.

The conversation of my hometown was no longer centered around its comfortable blue-collar, middle-class lifestyle, but rather what to now do with vast craters in the earth left by bulldozers and backhoes after removing the rubble of 131 years of financial stability and security for employees and their families.

The Fox Cities, however, have adapted and thrived in the challenging times. Change never comes easy, and for many, having to be retrained in new lines of work after twenty or thirty years in a mill was a humbling test of character, but the character of those who make up the Fox Cities has won out yet again. New industries made up of tech corporations and health-care giants have reshaped the landscape and reinvigorated the

Neenah from the clock tower in 1888, view looking north on Commercial Street. Paper mills can be seen on both sides of the thoroughfare along the river. *Courtesy of the Neenah Historical Society.*

Neenah from the clock tower present day, view looking north on Commercial Street. Paper mills have been replaced by modern office buildings and a parking ramp. *Courtesy of Scott Wittman Visual, 2014.*

economy, creating a diverse, educated population guiding the Fox Cities into the twenty-first century.

The past, however, is who we are; it's where we came from, and it's how we learned to address obstacles in our path and overcome them for a more prominent and prosperous future. It is therefore only to our detriment if we choose to forget it.

This book is not, nor is it meant to be, a comprehensive history of all that has been lost in the Fox Cities. There are many buildings, industries and the like, that do not make an appearance in this book, even many that the reader may have surmised prior would be in a publication such as this, and that is understood. What I have attempted to do is create a cohesive and coherent compilation of past eras of a place of which there have been many differing perspectives and interpretations, such as those reaping the fortunes of paper and lumber, to those who worked for them, the evidence of the physical presence of both rapidly being eroded by "progress."

As a researcher, much of the information gathered of times gone by is at the mercy of past chroniclers of the age, whom we all owe an impossible-to-pay-back debt of gratitude. However, oftentimes names, dates, addresses and so forth were not as readily fact-checked as today's technologies allow, so inaccuracies in such were not uncommon in past reporting, though I have done my best to verify or rectify any and all that appear in these pages.

Many people assisted in my plight to write this book, as no author ever goes it alone and there are far too many to name them all here.

First and foremost, however, a strong thank-you to John Rodrigue, my editor, whose guidance has been invaluable as I worked my way through this project. My first book may never have happened without his help.

The Fox Cities have a plethora of wonderfully talented and skilled historians and librarians, and the public library resources are first rate. Thank you to the staffs of the Neenah, Menasha, Oshkosh, Appleton, Kaukauna and Kimberly Public Libraries, with special thanks to Joe Bongers at Menasha and Corinne Herro at Kimberly, who assisted me with full access to their photo collections, and to Michael McArthur at Oshkosh for recommending several works that would've likely gone unnoticed by me.

Thank you, also, to Emily Rock at the History Museum at the Castle in Appleton and to Scott Cross at the Oshkosh Public Museum for their invaluable assistance obtaining photographs from their extensive and wonderful collections.

Thank you to Jane Azzi at the Paper Discovery Center in Appleton and Austin Frederick at the Winnebago County Historical and Archaeological Society for being incredibly gracious with their time and allowing me to search through the archives of the beautifully remodeled Atlas Mill and John R. Morgan residence, respectively, and providing me with their own wealth of knowledge about our area's heritage and history, and to Laura Fiser, curator of Collections and Exhibitions at the Paine Art Center in Oshkosh, for providing me access to the photo collections of the exquisite museum's extensive holdings.

Thank you to the local historical societies in the Fox Cities, who do a masterful job of preserving our heritage, specifically Jane Lang at the Neenah Historical Society; Christine Williams, Gwen Sargeant, and Dave Kalz at the Appleton Historical Society; and Mary Lamers at the Kimberly Historical Society for offering photos, knowledge and information for the completion of this work, as well as Erin K. Dix, university archivist at Lawrence University and Joseph R. Derose and Chad Matthew Thompson at the Wisconsin Historical Society for their assistance in obtaining photos.

Finally, two people who deserve special attention: Marge VanHeuklon, who reached out to me and introduced me to the work of her father, photographer Andrew J. Mueller, whose photographs are a treasure-trove of art and information and now rightfully reside in the collections of the History Museum at the Castle. I am proud to display some of his photos in this book. And George A. Whiting III, "Tripp," whose gracious offering of his family's private archives of the Whiting Paper Company proved invaluable to such a publication, and I am honored and humbled to have had the chance to study them.

THE SMILING VALLEY

On a hot midsummer day in July 1904, a reporter for the *Appleton Crescent* was on a hunt for a story. Only eighteen, and the first female reporter ever hired by the newspaper, she was on a quest to track down a celebrity she discovered was visiting this seemingly ordinary midwestern town. Being a woman, and fairly new on the job, she was used to having been bequeathed the more mundane news items of the day—the "crumbs," as she later referred to them—while having to sit back and watch as her male colleagues tackled the hard news current affairs people were talking about. This story, if her search was successful, could maybe be the one to get her the headlines for a change.

She crisscrossed College Avenue and the downtown area searching for the star. She checked the Sherman Hotel and the Appleton Theater, among other places she thought the person might be, but found nothing. Appleton, Wisconsin, a town of about sixteen thousand at the time, did not garner a lot of attention from the famous in 1904. Sightings of celebrities were few and far between, if they happened at all. Landing such an interview might convince her editor to pass along some of the more important stories to her in the future. This celebrity, however, didn't seem to want to be found.

Dispirited, she began her walk back to the Crescent Building at the corner of College Avenue and Morrison Street. While just across the street from her office, her eyes came upon a man standing outside a corner drugstore. The man was an "unassuming, pleasant faced, young fellow…interestingly dressed," with seemingly nothing about him out of the ordinary. After a

Lawrence University Main Hall, 1880. *Library of Congress*

glance, however, and then a second, the reporter quickly realized that she was not looking at just any ordinary man. She was, in fact, looking at one of the most famous people in the world. She had found her subject. His name was Harry Houdini.

As time would later prove, the reporter was also not just any ordinary reporter. Her name was Edna Ferber, and she would become one of the most accomplished novelists and playwrights in American history. Houdini granted Ferber her interview, which was published in the *Appleton Crescent* on July 23, 1904.

Houdini relayed to Ferber that he was in Appleton "looking up old friends," having lived here as a boy. Back then, he was simply Ehrich Weiss, son of Appleton's first rabbi. The interview provides a colorful scope into the would-be world-renowned escape artist's coming of age in Appleton. He talked affectionately of Appleton and his family. He reminisced about going to his father's offices above College Avenue, between Oneida and Morrison Streets, before construction of the Temple Zion, which his father commissioned. He talked openly with Ferber about various subjects,

The Crescent Building at the time Edna Ferber worked for the paper. Built in 1871 by William Waters at College Avenue and Morrison Street, originally for the Manufacturers Bank. Date razed, unclear. *Courtesy of the Oshkosh Public Library.*

including his travels, his earnings and even his remembrance, "as if it had taken place yesterday," of his first performance in front of an audience, which was in Appleton, "in an old field across the track in the Sixth ward."

The site where that conversation between Appleton's two best-known former residents took place looks a bit different today than in 1904. The corner drugstore has since been replaced by a modern law building. The Crescent Building, which stood across the street, has also succumbed to time, as the *Appleton Crescent* would later merge with its then competitor, the *Appleton Post*, to form the *Post-Crescent* of today.

Advertisement for Houdini at the Palace Theatre in Halifax in 1903, months before his meeting with Edna Ferber in Appleton. *Library of Congress.*

What was it about this area that kept drawing Ehrich Weiss, already by 1904 an acclaimed celebrity, back? What was it about Appleton that he so assertively referred to it as the place of his birth, even expressing that to Ferber, knowing he was actually born in Hungary, unbeknownst to anyone else at the time. Harry Houdini left Appleton when he was approximately nine years old, though he made sure Appleton remained a prominent part of his biography his entire life, even playing with facts to accentuate his connection to the city. Not until immigration records were uncovered in the late twentieth century did the rest of the world learn of Houdini's true place of birth.

The history of Appleton, and the Fox Cities, is as unique as the great escape artist himself. The meandering river that runs through it, giving the region its moniker, remains the lifeblood of a people prided on innovation, hard work and providing for families that have maintained that way of life for generations, each one leaving its mark on the next. Harry Houdini—or Ehrich Weiss—knew this. This is the place he wanted to be associated with. Appleton, and the "smiling valley in whose arms the town so contentedly nestled," as Ferber later referred to it, is where he wanted to go to be grounded after worldly travels. Ferber exquisitely relays this in her article.

As Houdini and Ferber have added their chapters to Appleton's early days, the town's beginnings are not without their share of colorful characters to add to its biography as well. Truth be told, there would be no Appleton without Lawrence University, which lies at its center—and there would be no Lawrence University without the antics of one Eleazer Williams.

The saga of Eleazer Williams actually begins in Europe in 1792, with the French Revolution in full force. King Louis XVI was stripped of his powers and imprisoned along with his queen, Marie Antoinette, their twelve-year-old daughter and seven-year-old son, the *dauphin*, or heir to the throne. Both king and queen were soon executed by guillotine, making the dauphin a king at eight years old. By 1795, the now boy-king was succumbing to the horrors of captivity. Abused, starved and forced to live in wretched conditions, his body soon developed a wrath of tumors, lesions and open sores. The official accounts state the boy died in captivity of tuberculosis at age ten.

Fast-forward to 1841, when a former American spy, Indian agent and missionary living in Green Bay, Wisconsin, named Eleazer Williams dropped a bombshell: he was the "Lost Dauphin," smuggled out of captivity in Paris as a young boy and secretly brought to America!

Williams's life was as eccentric as it was unbelievable. Raised by Mohawks in Canada, he claimed he had no memory of his life prior to age twelve, though he knew he was adopted as a child. After leaving the tribe to be schooled in Massachusetts, Williams went on to spy for the Americans during the War of 1812. Later, he became a religious leader among the Oneida under the Diocese of New York and was astonishingly successful in not only converting the Oneida to Christianity but also leading their migration west. Under his leadership, the Oneida and Stockbridge Indians settled on lands near Green Bay. Williams soon married, inherited through that marriage thousands of acres of land around present-day De Pere and settled on a homestead along the Fox River, where he dreamed of creating his own Indian empire. Over time, however, the Oneida felt Williams abandoned them, and he was ostracized by the tribes as well as the diocese.

Then, in 1841, the Prince de Joinville, son of Louis Philippe I, king of the French (and cousin to the supposedly dead boy-king) arrived in Green Bay and met privately with Eleazer Williams. Nobody knows exactly what was spoken about during this meeting, but according to Williams, this is when he was informed of his royal blood. Here he was told that as a child in captivity, he was smuggled out (with another sick child used as a stand-in) and brought to America, where he was adopted by a Native family—his Mohawk parents.

Williams was also asked to sign away his right to the throne in exchange for an array of riches. He refused.

The exiled Indian agent became a national celebrity. Soon, newspaper and magazine articles spread his story, as did several books supporting his claims. In due time, however, his popularity began to wane. Before long, dozens more came forward throughout the world also claiming to be the Lost Dauphin, draining his credibility. Rumors had been swirling in France since the revolution that the boy-king had somehow escaped captivity, providing an opening for pretenders and opportunists.

By 1844, due to a string of poor financial management decisions, Williams was broke. Abandoned by all those he tried to swindle with his wild claims, he traveled back east to look for assistance and soon encountered Amos A. Lawrence, a member of a wealthy Boston philanthropist family, who was eager to oblige. Intrigued at the possibility of owning land in the West, Lawrence made several loans to Williams, the would-be king utilizing five thousand acres of his land along the Fox River as collateral. He was never able to buy it back.

Lawrence was now ready to commence his vision of establishing a college in the West, presumably on his newly purchased land along the Fox River, in or around De Pere. The location chosen, however, was about fifteen miles south, in Grand Chute, where the river falls approximately forty feet in a few miles, making the potential for waterpower, and a possible future city that might feed off it, very enticing. Although it was not on the Williams land, Lawrence purchased the tract anyway and built his college. The city, as predicted, rose up around it.

Originally named the Lawrence Institute of Wisconsin, today's Lawrence University is one of the nation's leading liberal arts colleges, with an alumni list that runs parallel with the storied past of the Fox Cities. Familiar names, such as Kimberly, Paine, Bergstrom, Clark, Whiting and Grignon, among many others, add to an impressive list of former students who would go on to change the industrial world as they knew it.

Eleazer Williams eventually moved to New York, where he died in poverty and alone in 1858. But the mystery and debate over the "Lost Dauphin" would carry into the twenty-first century, when in April 2000, DNA taken from a small, dried-up and hardened human heart, said to have been ripped from the dead boy after his death and secretly saved for two hundred years, apparently proved the dauphin did indeed die in prison. Still today there are those who dispute the DNA tests, clamoring for their favorite imposter.

On the western banks of the Fox River in De Pere lies a small, nineteen-acre, rather unassuming tract of land. Although founded as a state park

Lawrence University's Underwood Observatory, built 1891 *(left)* and first Alexander Gym *(middle)* built 1901. Both razed in 1960s to make room for Youngchild Hall. *Courtesy of Lawrence University.*

in 1947, this quiet plot of land does not contain the natural wonders, observation towers or monuments of other state parks. It doesn't have cars lining up to enter its gates or waiting lists for reservations. What this park does have, however, is a history as unique and extravagant as any other. Although officially no longer a state park but still on state-owned land, Lost Dauphin Park, along Lost Dauphin Road, is what remains today of Eleazer Williams's failed empire.

Long before Eleazer Williams began scheming to become a king, a Native empire did exist in what is now the Fox Cities and ruled this area for several centuries. The Ho-Chunk (Winnebago) Nation was the preeminent regime of the western shores of Lake Michigan and throughout the Fox River Valley prior to European arrival and no comprehensive history of the Fox Cities, or Wisconsin, can be told without them. A Siouan-speaking people, they were known to the French to be in this area as early as 1616 and famously greeted Jean Nicolet at Red Banks in 1634. The Ho-Chunk also include the very first woman to ever be written about in Wisconsin's recorded history.

Her name was Hopokoekau, or "Glory of the Morning," and she remains, to this day, the only known female chief of the Winnebago/Ho-Chunk Nation, and quite possibly the subject of Wisconsin's very first documented love story.

The daughter of the Ho-Chunk chief, Glory of the Morning was born around the year 1711 in an island village located near the northern base of Lake Winnebago. The island, formed by two branches of the Fox River flowing out from Lake Winnebago, is today known as Doty Island and includes sections of Neenah and Menasha.

In her early years, Glory of the Morning made quite an impression on the tribe. Her wisdom, unusually superior, set her apart from others, including her brothers and the elders of the tribe. When she was eighteen, her father became ill and passed away, leaving the nation without a leader. In a stunning milestone event, Glory of the Morning was named to succeed her father as chief, causing a brief uproar by many in the tribe.

During her reign, the French became involved in the Fox Wars throughout present-day Michigan and Wisconsin. For France to continue building its empire in North America, the Fox River was vital for access to the Mississippi River and the western lands. The Fox River, however, was controlled by the Fox Indians, who were a deadly menace to the French. Surprise attacks and all-out slaughters were carried out by both sides, leaving a bloody, haunted history flowing through these waters.

Throughout the Fox Wars, as well as the years of the fur trade, many French Canadians passed through the region while serving their country's interests. One of these men was a French military officer named Joseph Sabrevoir Descaris, who, along with his men, established friendly relations with the Ho-Chunk on the island, ultimately culminating in Descaris's marriage to Glory of the Morning. The officer was so enamored by her and the island village that he resigned his commission in the French military and became a fur trader, remaining on the island with Glory of the Morning and her people.

Breaking with much of the Greater Ho-Chunk Nation, Glory of the Morning aligned with the French against the Fox Indians throughout the 1730s and '40s, though it was also largely her efforts that led to peace being established and an end to the wars.

In time, however, Descaris grew restless. His home country was facing a growing threat to its empire in North America from Great Britain, and he could not simply stand by. He was still a Frenchman, and with his country on the verge of war with its greatest European rival, he was again ready to

The typical attire of a Winnebago chief at the time of Glory of the Morning. *Library of Congress.*

be an officer. After seven years of marriage and fathering three children, Joseph Descaris left the island and returned to his French Canadian roots to re-enlist in the military and fight for his country. Glory of the Morning was torn. She understood the obligations of duty he felt for his people, as she felt the same for hers. Because of this, she decided to let Descaris go on without her, citing her refusal to leave her people without a leader. She did, however, offer for him to take their youngest child, a daughter, Nqno'abewiga. She would never see either of them again.

Years later, when the British invasion of North America was in full force and the French and Indian Wars were raging, Glory of the Morning remained loyal to her French Canadian husband and ordered her braves on the warpath against his country's enemy tribes. Their eldest son joined his father at the Battle of Sainte-Foy, a French victory reclaiming the city of Quebec from the British. It would be the last French victory of the French and Indian Wars.

Among the 833 French casualties of that day was Joseph Sabrevoir Descaris. Wounded in the battle, he died several days later. His son survived and returned to his mother. Their daughter remained in Canada, living out her days married to a French Canadian trader in Montreal.

Today, the Descaris name is still prevalent in the Ho-Chunk/Winnebago Nation, the pronunciation evolving over time, and is now known as the famed "Decorah" family. Their descendants thrived in a celebrated line of Ho-Chunk chiefs, including Spoon Decorah, Old Decorah, One-Eyed Decorah and Waukon Decorah. Their influence was instrumental in many of the treaties signed between various Native American tribes and the United States.

After 1766, Glory of the Morning disappears from written history—and astonishingly reappears in an account by famed nineteenth-century author Juliette Kinzie, who visited the tribe on the island while her husband was an Indian agent stationed at Fort Winnebago, near Portage, Wisconsin. Mrs. Kinzie describes the following encounter:

> *There was among their number, this year, one whom I had never before seen—the mother of the elder Day-kau-ray. No one could tell her age, but all agreed that she must have seen upwards of a hundred winters. Her eyes dimmed, and almost white with age—her face dark and withered, like a baked apple—her voice tremulous and feeble, except when raised in fury to reprove her graceless grandsons, who were fond of playing her all sorts of mischievous tricks, indicated the very great age she must have attained.*

The astonishing aspect is that this account illustrates a visit Mrs. Kinzie made to the island in 1832, when Glory of the Morning would have been approximately 121 years old! As there is no recorded date of her death, history can only believe what seems to be the unbelievable.

Four years after the Kinzie visit, in 1836, the Ho-Chunk, along with thousands of other Native Americans, mostly Menominee, were relocated west. In what is known today as the Treaty of the Cedars, at a site along the Fox River in present-day Little Chute, four million acres of land was signed over to the United States for just over $700,000, the ethics of which many of us tend to try and forget about today. This land included what is now the cities of Appleton, Neenah, Menasha, Oshkosh and Stevens Point, among others. The U.S. government took control of the land and subsequently sold the island to James Duane Doty, who proceeded to name it after himself.

Today, when walking along the rows of giant oaks and willows abundant throughout Doty Island, it's easy for one's imagination to overflow amongst the sound of water and light wind, the modern streets lined with mansions built by nineteenth-century paper barons, and the island's many parks, which hold their scenic beauty throughout any season. It's easy to imagine why the Ho-Chunk chose this place as their home centuries ago. And it's easy to imagine the spirits of two long-lost lovers, a forest queen and a military man, choosing to remain here together in death, companionship that war deprived them of in life.

Present at the Treaty of the Cedars and acting as an interpreter and negotiator for the U.S. government was Charles A. Grignon, son of the famed fur trader Augustin Grignon and great-grandson of frontier warrior Charles de Langlade, often referred to as the "Father of Wisconsin." As Grignon was also the grandson of a Menominee woman, he had an ideal skill set for a government interpreter and assisted at many treaties and traveled quite extensively for his duties, the most substantial of which was at the Cedars, which happened to be walking distance from his front door.

For decades prior to the Treaty of the Cedars, the Grignons were heavily active in the local fur trade along the Fox River. Wisconsin, and specifically the Fox River, was vital to the European demand for beaver pelts, which drove the economy of the Fox River Valley throughout the seventeenth and eighteenth centuries, and the river itself acted as a pipeline for the cash flow into the French Canadian territories. Because of this, control of the river became paramount, which led to decades of war between the native tribes, Great Britain and France.

To escape the bloodshed, Paul DuCharme sold his trading post, on land purchased by his brother Dominique from the Menominee in the first land deed ever recorded in Wisconsin, to Charles Grignon's father, Augustin. The land, called Kaukauna today, sat adjacent to three waterfalls formed by the river dropping about fifty feet in a mile, creating unpassable rapids and a natural portage. Augustin Grignon moved to the property in 1813, setting up his own trading post, gristmill and sawmill. By 1830, Augustin had moved with his wife to Butte des Morts, where he ran another trading post, leaving the land in Kaukauna to his eldest son, Charles, though by this time both the beaver and the wooded areas needed for trapping began to disappear and the fur trade era in Wisconsin was entering its demise.

To compensate for the lost income with the ending fur trade, Charles turned his attention to the growing interactions between whites and Native Americans and the need for interpreters, making use of his Menominee background to negotiate numerous treaties throughout his lifetime. For his work at the Treaty of the Cedars in 1836, he was paid $10,000, an exorbitant sum for the day. In 1837, on his father's old land, he built a mansion.

The Greek Revival home, known in its day as the Mansion in the Woods, had every bit of elegance seen in the wealthy cities of the East Coast in the early to mid-nineteenth century. The materials utilized to construct the mansion were shipped from New York, through the Great Lakes and down the Fox River, just in time for Charles's new Pennsylvania bride to make it her home. The house stood as a famous landmark for adventurers on the Fox River for many years, often providing hospitality and comfort to those exhausted from a lengthy passage. Many written accounts remain today depicting the neighborly treatment offered to them by Charles and his family. It was not unusual for the solo excursionist stranger to receive the same welcome at the Grignon home as a well-known dignitary, and the mansion attracted both.

The complete story of the Charles A. Grignon family, however, is somewhat of a tragic one. Although he was certainly unaware of it at the time, the Treaty of the Cedars, which Charles helped negotiate, essentially was the nail in the coffin of the fur trade on the Fox River and ended the century-long reign of the Grignons as the preeminent fur traders in the region. Charles entered the political arena, serving as Kaukauna's first town chairman and also as Outagamie County treasurer, along with his work as an interpreter, to continue to support his wife and their eleven children, only nine of which survived into adulthood.

Charles A. Grignon died unexpectedly at the age of fifty-four, leaving his widow, Mary Elizabeth, to care for and support their nine children, the last of whom was two months from being born at the time of Charles's death. Many of the children continued to live in the manor with their mother, assisting to support her and maintain the massive home. Such a task, unfortunately, was unrealistic, as the remaining family members struggled financially and the mansion began a slow demise into disrepair.

Grignon Mansion in disrepair in 1934. *Courtesy of the Kaukauna Public Library.*

Grignon Mansion after restoration, circa 1949. *Courtesy of the Kaukauna Public Library.*

Sadly, out of eleven children of their own, Charles and Mary Elizabeth only had two grandchildren, both of whom died childless. The last living resident of the mansion, the widow of the Grignons' tenth child, sold the home to Outagamie County in 1939. After delinquent taxes and other obligations were paid, she received only $231.75. Edith Acker Grignon, who for a time met tourists at the home after it became a museum, passed away in 1948. The Grignons of the Mansion in the Woods died with her.

The Grignon home has since undergone two restorations, and it now stands proudly as it did when Charles and Mary Elizabeth lived there.

Although Charles A. Grignon's family has no remaining descendants, the Grignon name remains throughout Wisconsin and the Fox River Valley. Many come from the family tree of Hippolyte Grignon, Charles's uncle and the first white settler in Appleton, who built his home along the Fox at what is now Lutz Park in 1835. One can stand today on the site of his home, which he named White Heron, and envision Appleton as it was during its frontier past. One can take in the scene and imagine why he built his home at this place, just under the bluffs from where Amos Lawrence would later build his college, and the surrounding city would create its downtown where two future residents would later have a chance meeting.

State historic marker at the site of the Treaty of the Cedars, Little Chute. *Courtesy of Scott Wittman Visual, 2018.*

In her autobiography, Edna Ferber would later recall that day with Houdini, writing:

> *Outside the store was the usual slot machine containing chocolate and chewing gum. As he chatted affably with me Houdini leaned carelessly against this. At the end of the interview he dropped a cold metal object into my hand.*
>
> *"There's a padlock to this slot machine," he said. "Better give it to the drugstore man. Somebody'll steal all the chewing gum."*
>
> *I hadn't seen so much as a movement of his fingers. Tottering with admiration I went back to my office to write my story.*

TURNING SAWDUST INTO GOLD DUST

At the close of business on Friday, August 9, 2009, seventy-nine employees at the Jeld-Wen Windows and Door Manufacturing Plant left their jobs for the last time and didn't know when their next paychecks were coming, or from whom. The last of the lumber companies, which harkened back to the days when the Fox River was lined with sawmills and wood shavings, had closed, ending an era that had given Oshkosh its identity for most of its existence.

In 1998, Jeld-Wen purchased Morgan Door, which was originally founded by pioneer brothers John R. and Richard T. Morgan almost a century and a half earlier. A hallmark of Oshkosh's early landscape with its mill buildings rising above the riverbank, Morgan Brothers was one of the early driving forces catapulting Oshkosh into its status as one of the leading wood-product manufacturers in the world. At one point in the late eighteenth century, Oshkosh numbered nearly sixty sawmills and wood product plants, taking on the moniker of "Sawdust City," as well as several other nicknames due to its lumberjacks, gambling halls and brothels. One by one, over a century and a half, the mills began succumbing to ever-changing economies and technologies, with Morgan Door being the last to hold on through its acquisition by Jeld-Wen, which proceeded to tear down the historic old buildings for a new sixty-five-thousand-square-foot facility in 2001, only to fall to the same sword, or wrecking ball, just eight years later.

It was no coincidence that soon after the Treaty of the Cedars was signed in 1836, lumbering developed into the next dominant industry in the

Morgan Brothers Lumber Company, corner of Sixth and Oregon Streets, Oshkosh. Complex razed in 2001. Circa 1887. *Courtesy of the Winnebago County Historical and Archaeological Society.*

Fox Cities. Millions of acres were opened for settlement, including much of the northern pine forests, which contained streams and rivers for easy navigation of cut logs down to the Fox and Lake Winnebago. With the first sawmill in the state's history being built by Augustin Grignon at his property in Kaukauna much earlier, by the 1840s, the Fox River was being utilized to power sawmills in Neenah and Menasha as well. It wasn't until around 1850 that the location advantages of the Fox River at Oshkosh, about fifteen miles south, were realized and taken advantage of.

Oshkosh had the luxury of the Wolf River, a Fox River tributary that makes its way north into the pine forests. The logs could be cut, marked and floated down the Wolf heading for the lumber mills along the Fox, which began rapidly increasing in numbers. Due to the rising number of different sawmills and lumber companies wanting in on the action, the logs coming from the north had to be identified and sorted to make sure they made their way to the specified owner. Hence Oshkosh's other big advantage, which was that it lay just to the east of two lakes, Lake Poygan and Lake Butte des Morts, which made for great boom bays of open water where the fleets of logs, sometimes miles long coming downriver, were sorted.

Horse-drawn sleds hauling raw cut logs down Commercial Street in Neenah, circa 1890s. *Courtesy of the Neenah Historical Society.*

As the rapid influx of settlers poured into the area, the thirst for lumber was insatiable. The need was endless for houses, barns, furniture and fuel, and Wisconsin had a never-ending supply, or so one thought, of white pine forests to fulfill the demand. White pine was the most sought-after raw material, as it was strong yet light enough in weight to be floated down the river to the mills in Oshkosh and beyond. For the next ninety years, Wisconsin pines would be made into windows, doors, shingles and sashes in homes throughout the state and the nation. The wood products would help furnish America's new cities in the West, rebuild Chicago after the Great Fire of 1871 and reconstruct the South after the Civil War.

As demand increased, workers were needed to work the lumber camps along with the mills, and immigrants from Europe poured in to heed the call. Germans, Irish, Poles, Norwegians and Welsh, as well as American easterners, rolled into the region, making Oshkosh the largest city in the Fox River Valley at the time, as well as the second-largest in Wisconsin. By 1890, the lumber industry employed nearly a quarter of all workers in the state.

Those workers made an indelible mark on Oshkosh's storied past. In the *Federal Writers' Project Guide to 1930s Wisconsin*, a federally commissioned comprehensive guidebook to each state's culture and heritage, a common scene in Oshkosh when the loggers returned from the northern forests is described as follows:

> *In these days the lumberjacks came roaring into town on pay day, stopping first at Otto Naus's Saloon at the foot of Main Street. Naus had three inches of sawdust on the floor to prevent their cleated boots from ripping it to pieces. The lumberjacks would work up the Main Street saloons, hire buckboards, and then invite their ladies to a keg of whiskey and some swimming in the river. The townsmen, having sold them supplies at high prices, would grumble tolerantly at the noise and fighting.*

Although Oshkosh was without question the hub of lumber activity in the Fox River Valley, the industry was not exclusive to the city. The first sawmills in the area were started along the river in Neenah, before the logistical advantages of Oshkosh were fully taken advantage of. These sawmills were the first in the area to explore the northern region and transport raw materials from the pineries. Henry Sherry, a Neenah resident, was among the wealthiest and most influential of all Wisconsin lumbermen, as he was ahead of the game and, anticipating the boom to come, bought up much of the virgin forest. It was largely his early successes in lumbering and subsequent financial viability that led to the development of Neenah's business district and stimulation of further industrial innovations, foreshadowing a very prosperous future for Neenah/Menasha.

In 1852, Elisha Smith purchased a small failing pail factory in Menasha, and turned it into Menasha Woodenwares, the largest producer of wooden pails, buckets, tubs and shipping containers in the nation. It still exists today as Menasha Corporation, one of the oldest privately owned family companies in the United States.

And the Kaukauna Lumber and Manufacturing Company was the first business in the nation to have an electrically operated sawmill, cutting the cord tethering the industry to water or steam power and proving Oshkosh's hold on lumber was not iron tight.

By 1900, Oshkosh's reputation, although exaggerated to be sure, was of a roughness much different than its neighboring Fox River Valley frontier towns to the north. Bar brawls, which soon morphed into prizefighting, were common, as were gambling, drinking and every other form of entertainment imaginable to men who worked twelve-hour days, six days a week in a logging camp or sawmill. Because of the high concentration of male workers, women followed. Lots and lots of single women. Most of

Kaukauna Lumber & Manufacturing Company, circa 1890. *Courtesy of the Kaukauna Public Library.*

Wieckert Lumber Co. planing mill, view facing south on tailrace of Fox River, 1885. *Courtesy of the Neenah Historical Society.*

these men were uneducated and largely unskilled, though they did what they needed to do as they tried to survive living outside of "the old country."

As immigrants saw the white pine forests as a job opportunity and a chance for survival, investors on the East Coast saw them as dollar signs. As the New England forests diminished, the eastern lumber magnates looked to virgin lands and the pineries of Wisconsin. Newspapers on the East Coast ran advertisements touting the financial opportunities, and loosened government regulations, for those willing to try their hand in the white pine frontier forests of the West. Of those who did, most, initially, failed.

The brutal harshness of the Wisconsin elements often sent the New England tycoons back with a loss. Their forests were burned up in fires. Their sawmills and dams were washed away in floods. The sheer remoteness of the pineries made getting supplies to the camps extremely difficult and excessively costly. Maiming and death were not infrequent among employees of the dangerous and virtually unregulated trade.

Those who persevered, on the other hand, wound up reaping the rewards. Desperate times created innovation, and by 1870 the industry had been completely modernized. From better hand tools, to dam building, to saw blades and log-hauling methods, lumbermen figured out how to sidestep Mother Nature and complete each task more efficiently and cost-effectively, propelling the industry into a gold mine for the lumber barons.

The real savior of the lumber industry, however, was the arrival of the railroads. With lumbermen no longer reliant on water levels to float logs to the booms to be sorted, the logs were now sent by rail to the sawmills to be worked and then shipped out to new markets not within reach in the days before the railroad. An entirely new timber resource was opened as well, as the usage of hardwood, which was too dense to be floated downstream but could now be sent via rail, came into play. Sawmills not on a railroad were now at a distinct disadvantage and ultimately closed up shop. Fortunately for Oshkosh, its rail system was one of the best north of Milwaukee and the sawmills there could barely keep up with demand.

One of those who made the trek west to Wisconsin was Connecticut-born Edward L. Paine, who worked in the lumber trade in Upstate New York until he set his sights on Oshkosh in 1853. In that year, he tore down his sawmill piece by piece, brought everything he could to the banks of the Fox River and set up shop in Oshkosh with his sons, Charles and George, turning the raw white pine into lumber and shingles. Because of its location along the water routes of the Fox River and Lake Winnebago and later along the rail lines, the company not only maintained but also prospered through the next two decades as many of its smaller competitors drifted off. Edward L. Paine retired in 1870 and turned the company over to his two sons, soon incorporating as the Paine Lumber Company Ltd.

As the logging industry began its decline, in no small part due to alternative building materials, such as brick, stone and steel, the Paines realized their survival depended on their ability to evolve as a business or they, too, would go the way of the fur trade. Charles and George turned their attention to the manufacturing of doors and built new factories on the Paine campus in the early 1880s. After Charles's death in 1885, it was George's turn to preside over the business and its transition from strictly lumber and shingles to doors, blinds and frames.

By 1908, the portable sawmill that Edward L. Paine picked up and moved to Oshkosh fifty years earlier was the largest and most successful sash and door company in the world.

The company continued to grow, even opening branches in other states, throughout the beginning of the twentieth century. A building boom after World War I increased demand even more, and at its peak in the late

Paine Lumber complex along Fox River, circa 1880s. *Courtesy of the Paine Art Center and Gardens.*

Sawmill at Paine Lumber Company, circa 1887. *Courtesy of the Oshkosh Public Library.*

1920s the Paine Lumber Company employed roughly 2,200 people. In Oshkosh, the Paine Lumber campus constituted roughly sixty acres of land, highlighted by an imposing four-story brick-and-stone, one-hundred-by-three-hundred-foot industrial complex.

Two years after Edward L. Paine first arrived with his sawmill, two Welsh-born brothers who had learned all they could about the industry building small houses and barns in Upstate New York also moved into Oshkosh. John and Richard Morgan began work at a planing mill in 1855, buying out the owner and starting their own operation a year later. Morgan Brothers, later known as Morgan Door, became one of the most successful of all lumber companies and one of the few to last into the twenty-first century.

The Morgan Brothers story is a harrowing one, though also one of perseverance and steadfastness in the wake of repeated tragedies resulting in losses of resources, capital and life. No less than five times, Morgan Brothers mills were destroyed by fire. Fires tended to happen in towns literally built on sawdust, but the brothers seemed particularly unlucky. Flames tore through the business in 1860, 1871, 1874, 1875 and again in 1895. Each time, the mills and factories were overwhelmed and obliterated. Each time, Morgan Brothers rebuilt, with renewed optimism.

Paine Lumber Company sash, door and blind factory with lumberyard, circa 1887. *Courtesy of the Oshkosh Public Library.*

Employees at Paine Lumber Company, circa 1900. *Courtesy of the Paine Art Center and Gardens.*

Millions of board feet of raw lumber were burned up in the infernos, the financial implications of which alone were enough to put most companies out of operation. The Morgans carried on, undeterred. The ashes of the worst one, however, known as the Great Fire of 1875, which started in the Morgans' lumberyard, changed Oshkosh forever.

Much of Oshkosh's downtown and business district was destroyed that day, April 28, 1875. The fire started at the wood piles of the Morgan mills. Soon, the dry wooden buildings were being consumed and disaster was imminent. Thomas Davis, a clerk at the mills, grabbed a fire extinguisher and ran into the main office to save the company's record books, but was "nearly roasted to death" according to an account in the *Baltimore Underwriter*, May 6, 1875, as the national media took notice. In his 1976 book *Prairie, Pines, and People: Winnebago County in a New Perspective*, Tom Chambers describes the scene this way:

> *Fifteen minutes after he had gone in, Davis staggered through the smoke and what was by now a virtual wall of flame. He fell to the ground, his clothes afire, his lungs heaving mightily for fresh air. As he lay prostrate, the others could see that the extinguisher was gone, but that his back bore the impressions of its straps. For where the straps had been, Thomas Davis' flesh was seared.*

Thomas Davis, a Civil War veteran, husband and father of three, died later that night. He was thirty-four. After that day, stone, mortar and brick changed Oshkosh's landscape forever.

By 1889, after almost thirty-five years of building a dynasty, John and Richard had satisfied their ambitions and sold their interests to sons J. Earl Morgan and Albert T. Morgan, as well as their nephew Thomas R. Morgan. The second generation of Morgan Brothers turned out to be much like the first. After a fire destroyed the business in 1895, they not only rebuilt, but also expanded and modernized, even branching out to help form the Morgan Lumber and Cedar Company of Foster City, Michigan.

Tragedy knew no bounds, however. On August 19, 1903, Thomas was walking in the Morgan lumberyard and was approached by a seemingly disgruntled employee. After a brief conversation, the subject of which is unknown, the employee pulled out a revolver and shot Thomas three times at virtual point-blank range. The motive of such a senseless act remains unclear, as the murderer chose to escape justice, hanging himself in his jail cell.

Still, for over a century after, the company prevailed. Whether as Morgan Brothers, Morgan Door, the Morgan Company or Jeld-Wen, what started out as a venture between two brothers in 1855 became synonymous with the lore of "Sawdust City" itself, until the doors finally closed for one last time on August 9, 2009.

For six decades, the lumber industry reigned in the Fox River Valley, mainly in, but not limited to, Oshkosh. It had the largest impact of any industry in the state economy for over half a century and through blood, sweat and innovation created the best crafted wood products the world had ever seen. The names of the lumber barons have become familiar to future generations throughout Oshkosh, and beyond. Names like Philetus Sawyer, who amassed a fortune in timber and had the unusual distinction of serving as a U.S. congressman and a U.S. senator. Names like J.P. Gould, of Gould Manufacturing, where toy designer Alexander Calder had his prototype wooden toys made in the 1920s—and they are still highly collectible today. Names like Isaac Stephenson and F.H. Libby and Radford and McMillan and Wood and many more whose mere mention recalls the days when lumber was king.

The mere mention of those names, however, does not always elicit romantic nostalgia and stories of rowdy lumberjacks and folk heroes. As the nineteenth century headed for a close, the lumber barons in Oshkosh had a big problem on their hands. This was not a problem with weather, or tools, or fire. This problem was with their own employees, and the rest of the country was watching.

By 1890, the lumber industry was the largest industrial employer in the state, totaling nearly twenty thousand workers, a quarter of the entire industrial workforce. However, because much of the workforce was made up of unskilled laborers, the per capita pay ranked only forty-sixth out of sixty-three counted industries. Earlier, by the 1870s, labor unions had noted the apparent suppression and started to keep an eye on the situation in Oshkosh, as it was the controlling force in the industry—and they set their sights on George Paine.

Nowhere was the difference in employee and employer more noticeable and striking than in Oshkosh. The employees, as stated previously, were mostly immigrants: German, Polish, English, Irish and Norwegian. They lived predominantly south of the Fox River, in the small houses and dirt roads of the "Bloody Sixth Ward," so called due to the struggles of daily living. Accounts of the interior of the houses describe bare floors and hardly any furniture. Meals consisted of rye bread and coffee, along with whatever

"Sawdust City" scene looking toward Lake Winnebago, circa 1885. The lumber often acted as tinder for a stray spark or flame. *Courtesy of the Winnebago County Historical and Archaeological Society.*

vegetables they were able to grow in their own gardens. Meat was a luxury not often afforded to them.

The owners of the sawmills, on the other hand, lived mainly on the north side of the river, in mansions designed by world-class architects, along picturesque Algoma Boulevard. Most of the mill owners by 1898 were second-generation owners, sons of the original lumber barons who turned Wisconsin's forests into a multi-billion-dollar timber empire. Nobody had more influence in Oshkosh by this time than George Paine, son of Edward L. Paine and the dominant player in the Fox River Valley lumber scene.

The Paines operated under a business model that provided the least amount of value to the laborer, who was basically viewed as a business expense easily replaced. This was replicated by the majority of mill owners in Oshkosh, making the average wage for a male laborer in the Fox River lumber industry just $0.98 per ten-to-twelve-hour day, as opposed to the national average of about $2.75. Paine, apparently still thinking that wage was too steep, hired women and children to work in the mills in place of men at a fraction of a male's meager earnings.

The labor struggles in Oshkosh were beginning to be noticed by national organizations. A labor journal in 1894 indicated collusion between the mill owners had forced wages to a "starvation level." Upon seeing a report that

Oshkosh was the lowest wage-earning city for woodworkers in the country, and also employed more women and children than any other industry in the nation, Thomas Kidd, a woodworkers union leader and organizer affiliated with the American Federation of Labor (AFL), began meeting with the Oshkosh workers. In early 1898, Kidd consulted and educated the local leaders about the bargaining process and attempted to put pressure on the mill owners by increasing media coverage of their treatment of their employees. The Oshkosh workers took a vote and united under a Woodworkers' Council, which was recognized by the AFL, and the threat of a strike was now looming.

Paine, Morgan, McMillen and other owners were undeterred. After repeated broken promises and attempts to engage in discussions, the workers, under the guidance of Kidd and the support of the AFL, offered one last list of requests to the mill owners. The requests were for higher wages, an end to the use of women and children for labor, weekly pay and union recognition. George Paine threw the list in the wastebasket. No other mill owner so much as offered a response. At 7:00 a.m. on Monday, May 16, 1898, the Oshkosh Woodworkers' Strike began.

Employees at Paine Lumber Company with superintendent watching on, circa 1900. *Courtesy of the Paine Art Center and Gardens.*

The mill owners remained unmoved. They had agreed to work together to not give in to demands and began recruiting workers from outside of the area to keep their mills running. George Paine imported a group of Volga Germans, ethnic Germans who had historically lived along the Volga River in Russia, to work in his factories and housed them in company-owned row houses that he had built specifically for this reason. Over the next several decades, many of the family members of these immigrants joined them in Oshkosh and worked for the Paine Lumber Company well into the twentieth century, settling on the west side of the city and creating a large German contingent whose descendants remain today with familiar names like Wagner, Lautenschlager, Fischer, Koch and Hartmann. Other mill owners recruited workers out of southern Wisconsin and Chicago for replacement labor.

After the sixth week of the strike, the four biggest mills in Oshkosh—Paine, Morgan, McMillen and Radford—continued churning out enough product using "scabs" to meet market demands and keep the money rolling in. There was no sign of movement on their part at all.

The strikers, in a calculated move, but still one out of desperation, began a plan of harassment directed at the replacement workers. Some of the male strikers were too aggressive and wound up getting arrested for various offenses, draining the funds provided by the AFL to pay for bail and court costs instead. Fists, knives, clubs and the occasional gun were becoming more and more common during spats between replacement workers and union members, although heavy violence was initially kept at bay, for the most part.

Because of this, women and young boys were utilized to do the harassing in place of men, as they were much less likely to get arrested. Mass demonstrations were planned at each of the four remaining operating mills to terrorize the strikebreakers. As the scabs came and left work, they were pelted with rotten eggs, had salt and pepper thrown in their eyes and were taunted with clubs. Their objective worked, as Morgan and Radford announced they were closing until the "riots" were over.

The next day, the strike took a drastic turn and descended into chaos. As replacement workers were about to leave the McMillen mill at the close of the work day, they were greeted by approximately one thousand angry women and male teenagers, waiting outside the gate, ready for their attempt to shut down their next mill. The workers, frightened for their safety, picked up stones and loose lumber as they waited by the mill doors to make the walk home. The scene was set for a melee, and a melee ensued.

The mill engineer, Edward Casey, in a demonstration of inexplicable judgement, grabbed the company fire hose, opened the hydrants and pummeled the demonstrators with a hard rush of cold water. The swarm of picketers ripped the fence gate down and engulfed the courtyard of the mill, clashing with the replacement workers. Stones, lumber, sticks, fists and eggs were strewn carelessly about.

Within only a few minutes, the strikebreakers took cover back inside the building and the demonstrators controlled the mill yard—at one big cost: Jimmie Morris, a painter at Paine and assembling with the strikers, lay dying on the ground, clubbed in the back of the head. He was sixteen years old. The mob pointed their fingers at Casey, accusing him of murdering the boy. Later newspaper accounts surmised that Morris was killed accidentally by other strikers. Nobody can say for sure.

Again, however, the goal of the demonstrators was reached. McMillen and Paine closed down operations. The owners would put up with no more. The National Guard was called in the next day, and Gatling guns were set up around the city, an open warning to anybody who was looking to cause trouble.

Thomas Kidd, the union leader and organizer of the strike, was arrested and tried with conspiracy. He was defended by famed Chicago attorney Clarence Darrow in what turned out to be one of the most important cases ever adjudicated regarding labor relations in U.S. history.

Darrow was masterful in his defense, comparing the mill owners to prison wardens and eloquently describing the plight and fight for everyday survival of the Oshkosh woodworker and his family due to excessively harsh treatment by George Paine, Thomas Morgan, Robert J. McMillen and other tycoons.

Kidd was acquitted, as was Edward Casey, who was tried outside of the area. Jimmie Morris's funeral was described by publications of the day as having the largest attendance of any funeral in Oshkosh's history. He is buried an in unmarked grave at Riverside Cemetery.

By the turn of the twentieth century, the lumber industry as Oshkosh knew it was in steady decline. The white pine forests, once thought to be virtually inexhaustible, were cut over in less than sixty years. Focus turned to the manufacturing of wood products, which is where Oshkosh mills made their money. That, too, had a shelf life, and the crash of 1929 did most of them in.

George Paine died in 1917, leaving operations of his empire to his son, Nathan, who subscribed to much of the same philosophies as his father had

Employees at Paine Lumber Company, 1899, one year after the strike had ended. *Courtesy of the Paine Art Center and Gardens.*

in regard to business operations and labor costs, even erecting a thrift bank to keep all banking costs in-house and to attempt to profit off of the savings accounts of his own employees. The bank failed, and the building was later used as Paine offices. The building remains at 1621 Congress Avenue and is still today the best example of neoclassical architecture in Oshkosh. The crash of 1929 spared nobody, and Paine was no exception. The business was hit hard and closed in 1934, though Nathan reopened again three years later and lived out his days as company president, dying in 1947.

Paine Lumber lingered on for several more decades with various owners until forced into involuntary bankruptcy in 1983, at the time the nation's oldest manufacturer of wooden doors. By then, the Paine campus was more of an eyesore than an asset to the city. Occupying sixty acres of prime riverfront real estate, the buildings looked every bit of their seventy-five years and counting. Warehouses, powerhouses, woodworking shops and a water tower were tattered, bruised and abandoned, the mammoth manufacturing plant a withering remnant of the city's past glory.

Redevelopment of the land began in 1986, when the entire campus was razed except for the four-story industrial complex. That building, erected by George Paine in 1908, with twenty-eight-inch-thick walls and sixteen-by-sixteen-inch columns throughout, remains today as luxury condominiums, towering over the present-day restaurants and marinas that have replaced all the old buildings of the former lumber mecca, providing the largest of the few remaining vestiges of a past empire of pine.

The row houses George Paine had built for the Volga German replacement workers during the strike remain as well. Nathan had the row houses rebuilt in 1925 and utilized the buildings for employees who were newcomers to the area to rent until housing of their own was afforded. Today, the row houses are rented like any other modern townhouse, their link to Oshkosh's past industrial paternalism now found only in history books.

As a walk along the river district where the lumber kings once reigned will prove, little remains today of Oshkosh's lumber days. Jeld-Wen's closing in 2009 was the last breath for an era that began when Martin Van Buren was in the White House.

1908 Paine Lumber manufacturing plant, now modern luxury condominiums. The only building remaining from the Paine Lumber industrial campus. *Courtesy of Scott Wittman Visual, 2018.*

Paine Row Houses, circa 1930. Built to house Volga Germans in 1898. *Courtesy of the Paine Art Center and Gardens.*

The old Morgan Brothers mills, two three-story buildings on either side of Oregon Street at Sixth Avenue, were torn down by Jeld-Wen in 2001 in the name of efficiency. Costs to maintain the old buildings were said to be prohibitive, and the buildings were consolidated into one new sixty-five-thousand-square-foot facility. The site where Morgan Brothers once stood was, at the time, targeted for upscale residential use.

Jeld-Wen shut down eight years later, taking the new facility with it. That site, too, was targeted for a mix of upscale residential and commercial use. As of 2018, the site, which seemingly would be high-demand riverfront property, lies barren, a monumental empty hole in the heart of a once thriving district.

As is Pioneer Drive, just to the east of the former Morgan site, winding along the same riverbank once blanketed by the dust of sawmills and lines of smokestacks, now gone. Gone, too, is the constant whine and hum of blades cutting into raw pine which could be heard for miles. Vast swaths of

Present site of Morgan Brothers Lumber/Jeld-Wen, empty since 2009. Modern luxury apartments rise in the background. *Courtesy of Scott Wittman Visual, 2018.*

nothingness lie dormant along this once vibrant riverfront in place of what used to be a sea of logs, along with the former Pioneer Resort and Marina, which sits at the mouth of the river at Lake Winnebago, abandoned since the early 2000s.

Main Street also no longer gets invaded by hordes of lumberjacks fresh out of the forests for the first time in months, looking for anything and everything to help them forget where they just came from. High-rise luxury apartments and condominiums have taken their place, as well as a more cosmopolitan nightlife than anyone from the Bloody Sixth Ward could've ever imagined.

The names from the "Sawdust City" era remain prominent and familiar, almost ghost-like, but the businesses they ran are now only a memory.

The building at R. McMillen & Company, where the strike of 1898 turned deadly, remains. Starting as a sawmill in 1864 by Robert H. McMillen, who began in business with the Morgan Brothers before branching out and competing with them, it closed in 1942, never recovering from the Depression. The building was purchased then by Wisconsin Axle, now known as AxleTech, who coincidentally just went through their own employee strike in 2017, albeit much less contentiously.

In 1892, McMillen gave a slight foreshadow to what was to come in the Fox Valley in a quote published in the *Oshkosh Northwestern*. Choosing not to run his sawmill in Oshkosh that year due to decreasing profits, McMillen alluded to the fact that lumbering was on the downslope. "I feel as though I would just a soon clear up my business in this city entirely. I am now heavily

Abandoned Pioneer Resort and Marina along Pioneer Road, Oshkosh. *Courtesy of Scott Wittman Visual, 2018.*

Smokestack at Abe Rochlin Park at site of first operating sawmill in Oshkosh. *Courtesy of Scott Wittman Visual, 2018.*

interested in paper mills at Appleton, and we are to build another paper mill this summer, and I will devote more of my time to that business."

James P. Gould began what became Gould Manufacturing in 1869. During the strike, it was Gould who was always referred to as treating his employees with the most respect, even causing his employees hesitation to join the effort in the first place, though for the greater cause they did. James died in 1925, and in 1927, Gould Manufacturing signed a contract to produce wooden toys for an up-and-coming young toy designer named Alexander Calder. The line of toys was such a commercial success that Gould decided to halt the manufacture of all other wood products to focus solely on toys. Then came 1929. They, too, never recovered. Alexander Calder went on to become a world-renowned toy maker and sculptor whose work is highly sought after today.

There is, however, one final smokestack still standing along the Fox River in Oshkosh. On the site that was once the Paine veneer plant, a tall chimney stands alone, seemingly out of place as it now resides in a park of greenspace and playgrounds. The smokestack was from a later factory, a Pulswood plant that closed in the 1980s, and has a plaque attached to it recognizing the Oshkosh woodworker. Before Paine built here, another company did the same—in 1847. It was on this ground that Forman & Bashford sawed the first foot of lumber ever in Sawdust City.

VALLEY OF THE PAPER KINGS

Heading west off Tayco Street and along the old Government Canal in Menasha, winding past industrial buildings and over ancient-looking railroad tracks, River Road dead-ends where the Fox River opens into Little Lake Butte des Morts. There, standing as it has for the last 136 years, is the mill of the George A. Whiting Paper Company, a fixture of the local Fox Cities industrial scene since 1882. The site is minus the normal activity levels that had been customary here, as the buildings now stand idle and empty, closed in March 2016.

The first thing that hits you when you gaze at the property today is the silence. Gone is the hustle and bustle of employees coming and going. The roars and whines of iron machines churning out rolls of various specialty papers have given way to the soft sounds of birds and the occasional carried voice from the nearby Friendship Trail. Wooden pallets lie stacked on the grounds, a light remains on outside the loading dock and air conditioners adorn the round-arched windows of the redbrick, single-story, Georgian Revival office building, showing apparent signs of life, but they are merely artifacts of a once thriving, generational family-owned business.

In many ways, George A. Whiting's story is a microcosm of the broader saga of the paper industry in the Fox River Valley. No industry—not lumber, not flour, not the fur trade and nothing since—has had even close to the impact, economically, environmentally, socially or otherwise, on the Fox Cities as did the makers of paper. The same could be said for the loss of the industry.

The Whiting structures stand as a reminder of an industrial age that transformed the Fox Cities, their land, people and history forever; of how a river was conquered and harnessed and made to relinquish more power than any stretch of water in the world; and how the Fox River Valley created an empire of paper and changed the ways of the world, until the world changed it.

From a curious missed opportunity, to launching a self-taught industrial dynasty, to what is now becoming an all-too-familiar end, the story of the Whiting Paper Company, and the "Paper Valley" in general, is one rich with the American dream, but rooted in Fox Cities lore.

Papermaking in the United States has its beginnings in New England in the late seventeenth century. Benjamin Franklin became its biggest investor and advocate as he established numerous paper mills and printing presses throughout the colonies, as well as becoming a dealer in rags, which were

Overhead view of Whiting Paper Mill, circa 1940. *Courtesy of the Whiting family private collection.*

old cotton cloths and linens utilized to make paper in America's early years. Papermaking in the thirteen colonies, however, was an extremely laborious process, incurring many hours of tedious hard work and toil, exacerbating costs and failing to keep up with demands. Because of this, as well as a persistent shortage of rags, linens and other raw materials, paper shortages were common.

After the American Revolution, for which the importance of paper used as a communicative tool cannot be understated, paper mills began to move west along with the ever-growing and expanding nation. Although paper mills were becoming more in number, the processes remained the same, and the shortages continued, especially the farther away from the East Coast one was. In 1849, the Connecticut River was dammed at Holyoke, Massachusetts, creating enough waterpower to sustain a stream of rag paper able to meet demands in the region, and the area became the world's largest producer of paper toward the latter part of the eighteenth century.

It would soon have competition.

By 1847, paper shortages in the Midwest caused numerous newspapers to either cut back editions or halt production altogether, including the *Milwaukee Sentinel and Gazette*, one of the precursors to today's *Milwaukee Journal Sentinel*, which pleaded for a papermaker to set up shop in Wisconsin, still a territory at that time. The next year, the Ludington and Garland Company began making newsprint and wrapping paper in Milwaukee, the first paper ever manufactured in Wisconsin. The mill was in constant financial difficulty, changed hands several times and was never profitable.

A former employee of the Milwaukee mill, Charles Richmond, moved to Appleton in 1853 after the mill and its equipment were sold and the building demolished. Richmond soon partnered with an extended family member, Edwin Atkinson, to finance and build the first paper mill in the Fox Cities, purchasing machinery from an old mill in Chicago and transporting it by steamboat to their mill along the Fox River in Appleton. Within months, they were feeling the pinch for raw materials and felt propelled to plead with local farmers to bring them rye and oat straw to continue producing paper, offering to "pay a good price" to those who obliged—and oblige they did.

By 1854, Charles Richmond had bought out Atkinson and was now the sole owner of Appleton Paper Mills, producing book and wrapping papers. Due to a request by the *Appleton Crescent*, Richmond, now joined by his brother Norman, also began producing newsprint, although the *Crescent* saw fit to explain in its own pages the reason for the "rough" finish, and eventually found other suppliers.

The Richmond Brothers, however, were now on the national papermaking scene and began recruiting skilled craftsmen and paper artisans from the East Coast to join them in the Fox Valley. In an 1882 edition of the New York–published *Paper Trade Journal*, in an article also claiming Appleton as "fast becoming the papermaking centre of the west," it was noted that the "Richmond Brothers are running their mill to its full capacity on straw wrapping and bogus manila. They are the oldest manufacturers in the valley and sustain the reputation they long ago established."

The reason the Fox Valley was attractive to easterners and immigrants looking for industrial opportunity had everything to do with the river that runs through it. From Neenah, flowing north to De Pere, the Lower Fox River drops over 170 feet, approaching the height of Niagara Falls, in less than forty miles. In the mid-eighteenth century, rushing, falling water meant power, and the people of the Fox Cities were about to harness that energy quicker and more efficiently than anywhere else in the world.

By 1872, the birth of the "Paper Valley" was imminent. Here, eastern capitalists came in droves—hungry, determined and aggressive. Here was a river ready to power any industrial apparatus shown to her, be it made of wood, iron or stone. Here was a population ready to work and learn and grow in numbers. Here were experienced papermakers, honing and advancing their craft. And here, just north of the valley, were the vast forests forbidden by the lumbermen of pine, still standing tall, prepared to relinquish their possessions and aid in the innovative transition from rags and straw to wood pulp.

The Richmond Brothers Paper Mill would not live to see this technological advancement from rags to wood pulp riches. Their first mill, located right about where the remains of the Atlas Mill and Paper Discovery Center stand today, burned in 1859, an end seemingly almost destined to wooden buildings in early manufacturing and industry. Undaunted, they rebuilt, a mile downriver. The second mill remained highly successful, though it burned as well in 1886. The brothers, now older and ready to leave the grind behind, retired and sold the land to the Manufacturing Investment Company. A new mill was built in 1888, eventually becoming the Interlake Paper Mill and then a division of Consolidated Papers in 1916.

Panoramic scenes casting rows of raw lumber and bellowing smokestacks dominated the landscape there for decades, as the mill produced sulfite pulp for use in papermaking in other Consolidated mills throughout the state, as well as on the open market.

Consolidated Papers–Appleton Division, circa 1948. Erected in 1886 on the site of the Second Richmond Mill, it was razed in 1984. *Courtesy of the Andrew J. Mueller Collection at the History Museum at the Castle.*

The *Appleton Evening Crescent* described the local industry in 1901:

> *The big sulphite pulp mill of the Interlake Pulp and Paper Co., in Appleton uses…when running full force, one hundred cords of spruce and hemlock wood per day. This means ten car loads and is the average product of two and one-half acres of well-grown pulp timber.*
>
> *As the Fox River Valley is the center of the trade in the state, so Appleton is the center of the valley, and a very large percentage of this enormous trade is transacted through the Appleton offices of the various companies having their headquarters here.*
>
> *Here also is the center of the building trade which has erected these mammoth plants throughout the state, the architects who have planned and superintended the construction of the various plants, with very few exceptions, being located here.*

By the 1960s, however, the mill began to show its age. In 1968, the Department of Natural Resources gave all the mills along the Fox River until December 31 of that year to meet standards for the purpose of reducing pollution in the river. As many of the mills were in excess of eight decades old by that time, extensive renovations were often necessary. These regulations nearly led to the closing of the Appleton Consolidated mill in the early 1970s, as it struggled to comply with the new standards. A $14 million upgrade to the facility was needed to save it at that point, only to eventually fall victim again to changing technologies. The mill's parent company eventually converted to producing enamel papers for magazines, becoming the largest producer of such papers in the world. The Appleton site's pulp process was not compatible with such a product, however, forcing the corporation to purchase pulp somewhere other than its own pulp-making facility.

Due to the mill's age and ninety-year-old Mitscherlich pulping process it was originally fitted for, the facility and its almost two hundred employees were again at a crossroads. The open market for pulp had already begun to slow by the 1980s and would not be sufficient alone for the mill in Appleton to survive. If the mill could not be cost-effectively refitted for compatibility with its own enamel papermaking machines, it would simply become obsolete. Operations at the facility were suspended in April 1982 for experimental purposes to determine whether such a recalibration could be done to the old mill while remaining in compliance with DNR regulations. The tests were not encouraging.

On August 2, 1982, George Mead, the grandson of the man who purchased the mill in 1916, announced its closing after ninety-four years. "This combination of loss of outside markets and environmental demands creates an economic situation that we cannot overcome. No one wants Appleton's pulp at the price we need to make a profit. It is a losing operation that we can no longer tolerate."

Two years later, Consolidated Papers–Appleton Division was razed. The site along the Fox River once occupied by the first ever papermakers in the Fox River Valley sat abandoned for years, though now showcases a community of luxury apartments, restaurants and recreational trails.

By the time of the Richmond Mill's second fire, the floodgates had opened, and the Fox River Valley was in the midst of becoming the largest paper producer in the world. An 1872 meeting of five men in Neenah would cement that legacy forever.

Charles B. Clark, a twenty-eight-year-old Civil War veteran who noted the profits of both the Richmond Mill and the Neenah Paper Mill, which was begun seven years earlier, discussed a proposition with four of his friends in Neenah, none of whom had any papermaking experience, about opening their own mill. Each would put up a predetermined amount of capital and utilize its unique business expertise to begin the venture. Within a few weeks of that meeting, the Fox River Paper Mill Company was born, organized by Clark, John A. Kimberly, Frank Shattuck, Havilah Babcock and George A. Whiting. One month later, the business was reorganized into an equal partnership of Kimberly, Clark, Babcock and Shattuck, with Whiting omitted.

The four men quickly purchased and razed an old flour mill on the Fox River in downtown Neenah and built the Globe Mill, just to the west of the old Reliance Flour Mill. By October 1872, the Globe Mill had begun operations. Kimberly, Clark & Company, without George A. Whiting, would go on to become one of the largest manufacturers of paper the world has ever seen. It is not fully clear as to why George Whiting was left out. Written accounts of various historians have differed, some saying Whiting wanted too much control or that his age was a factor, as he was only twenty-three at the time, much younger than Babcock, Shattuck and Kimberly, who were

RiverHeath Apartment Community now occupies the former site of the Interlake-Consolidated Paper Mill along the Fox River in Appleton. *Courtesy of Scott Wittman Visual, 2018.*

in their mid-thirties. Both are mostly untrue, with the logical reasoning that Whiting simply didn't yet have the capital necessary to enter in to such an undertaking being the most likely case.

The Globe Mill was immediately successful. It hired away the foreman from the Neenah Mill, Myron Haynes, and was soon capable of producing two tons of superior quality printing paper every day, an impressive number for the times. Two years later, the company bought the mill that Haynes used to work for, too.

In 1890, the *Appleton Post* described the Globe's specialty as "Patent Bronze or Gold Papers and Relief Fibre Cuesta. The trailing of the fine vines in lines of gold interspersed with all the shades of the rainbow as they run off the machines into rolls of wall paper is certainly a curious sight."

By 1884, K-C was ready for expansion and built a new mill, the Badger, on the east side of the Reliance Flour Mill, eventually purchasing that facility as well, turning three mills into one mammoth facility as operations continued to outgrow their space. The new facility, known as the Badger-Globe Mill, turned out product for the next 115 years.

Here, in the Badger-Globe Mill, was the birthplace of Kimberly-Clark, and therefore it was here that the fate of the Fox Cities for the next century and a half was formed. Here some of the most familiar American brands ever known came into existence, brands like Huggies, Kotex and Kleenex.

In 1997, Kimberly-Clark, by then a behemoth Fortune 100 company, purchased Scott Tissue, expanding a global empire though, at the same time, commencing a company "restructuring," of the kind that usually leads to site consolidation. This would be no different. Announcing that eighteen plants would be closed throughout the country, Kimberly-Clark dropped a bomb on its hometown when it said the Badger-Globe Mill would be one of them.

In November 1998, the wreckers came for the Badger-Globe. Although Kimberly-Clark said at the time that the buildings had been altered so much over the decades that the mill complex had lost its historical significance, in reality, the company demolished quite probably the most historically significant structures the Fox Valley had ever known, and possibly ever will.

In 1878, continued expansion saw Kimberly-Clark join three Minnesota businessmen and build the Atlas Mill along the Fox River in Appleton. According to the *Appleton Post* at the time, the Atlas was the largest mill of its kind in the west, built of brick with a stone foundation, and there was "none in the whole country having a greater capacity." The mill was built on the site of a former sawmill and not far from where the Richmond Brothers original

Original Globe Mill erected by Kimberly-Clark in 1872. Razed in 1997. *Courtesy of the Neenah Historical Society.*

Globe Mill employees, circa 1880. *Courtesy of the Neenah Public Library.*

mill began operations. Always looking ahead, K-C also purchased additional buildings and land adjacent to the Atlas, and within the next several years three more paper mills were built, enlarging the already growing corporate colossus. The Tioga and Vulcan Mills were erected for producing book paper, and the Telulah Mill for high-grade newsprint. Another large mill was erected on the opposite side of the river, connected to the Atlas by a bridge, in which pine and poplar were ground into pulp.

On the morning of June 9, 1888, a fire started in the basement of the Atlas Mill. Within minutes, the flames shot up an elevator shaft and into the rag room, surging like a furnace and engulfing the premises. Within an hour, the facility was in ruins. Fortunately, the wind on that day was almost nonexistent and the flames never did penetrate a path to the neighboring Tioga, Vulcan or adjacent Appleton Pulp and Paper Company mills, otherwise the day could've been devastating to Appleton's industrial future.

J.A. Kimberly and Charles Clark had left the mill just a few hours prior to travel out of town, and the *Appleton Crescent* reported the fire before the owners likely even had heard about it, surmising, "It is presumable to suppose that they will immediately rebuild and on an extended scale." The paper was right. Not accepting the possible crippling blow to its bottom line, Kimberly-Clark rebuilt in just five months, increasing the already unmatched capacity from twenty-five tons to thirty-five tons of wrapping paper per day.

For the next 110 years, the Atlas was the site of some of the most revolutionary advancements in papermaking. The first paper in the state made from ground wood pulp was made at the Atlas, and numerous accomplishments in the growth and improvement of paper chemistry were conducted at the mill. For the first half of the twentieth century, the Atlas was the nation's leading producer of decorative wallpapers, along with producing various papers for specialty markets.

Beginning in the 1970s, however, the Atlas Mill began running a race against time. Bigger and faster mills came on line, and the Atlas was struggling to keep up with market demands. The facility seemed antiquated against modern mills, ironic for a mill in which were created the processes so imperative to the industry's future prominence. By 1987, the Atlas had shut down many of its operations and culled its workforce to about twenty-five hands. The end came for good in 1999.

For almost 130 years, the Badger-Globe and Atlas mills stood sentinel over a company and a community that evolved together from infancy, impacting the world and virtually every person in it. Within a span of two years, both were gone.

Mills on the Fox River in Neenah, circa 1890. *Library of Congress.*

The Vulcan Mill, although being one of the three buildings lighted in Appleton on September 30, 1882, by the world's first hydroelectric central power station, led a much less decorated and shorter lifespan, as did the Tioga Mill adjacent to it. In 1894, the *Crescent* was already reporting plans were in place by Kimberly-Clark to raze the mills and replace them with a new mill with a larger capacity than both older mills combined, as well as more job opportunities. Both mills were, indeed, dismantled in 1908 by Kimberly-Clark, though no new Appleton paper mill was yet built. Again in 1910, calling the Atlas Mill "old and out of date," the *Post-Crescent* surmised that the demolition of the Vulcan and Tioga Mills must only be succeeded by the construction of a larger mill to replace them, claiming, "It may be safely stated that it is but a matter of time until this big company will own and operate in Appleton one of the finest mills in Wisconsin."

Kimberly-Clark never did build that mill in Appleton. The Vulcan and Tioga Mills were replaced with the Vulcan Hydroelectric Plant, which provided electricity for the Atlas Mill as well as the Kimberly Mill, built in 1889. The power plant, massive for its day, ceased operations in 1974, lying dormant for decades until being restored into Fratello's Waterfront Restaurant in 2003 after much debate on potential redevelopment of the site.

The Telulah Mill was eventually sold to the Fox River Paper Company in 1920, and part of it still stands today, incorporated into the operations of the current Neenah Paper Inc.

By 1886, Kimberly-Clark's daily output of product was around seventy tons in book paper, wrapping paper and newsprint. No paper company within hundreds of miles could come close to that number. Yet, the four partners were looking to expand yet again to meet further demands.

In 1889, they chose a new millsite along the Fox River three miles east of Appleton, in what was basically a wilderness. There was no town, no houses and no community to speak of. They hired the leading paper mill architect of the time from Holyoke, Massachusetts, and designed a twenty-five-ton ground-wood pulp mill, a thirty-ton sulfite pulp mill and a ten-ton straw wrapping paper mill. They also built an entire residential and business community around the millsite for employees to relocate to. The community was complete with roads and sidewalks, a hotel, sixty houses and additional open lots. The Village of Kimberly, Wisconsin, named for John Alfred Kimberly, was born.

Telulah Paper Mill, circa 1890. *Courtesy of the Appleton Public Library*

George Whiting was not discouraged after being left out of the Kimberly-Clark reorganization. Three years after his omission, in 1875, Whiting purchased an interest in the Winnebago Paper Mill in Neenah, serving also as company secretary. Soon after, he became the manager of the mill and learned the craft and business of papermaking on the job. In 1878, it was Whiting who carried out the production of the first book paper in the region at the Winnebago Mill, two years before Kimberly-Clark.

By 1882, Whiting was growing restless again and looking for a new adventure to begin his own enterprise. He met and entered into a business partnership with the son of a paper dealer from Philadelphia, William Markley Gilbert, and the two opened their own paper mill. Gilbert & Whiting Paper was an instant success, which made both men's ambitions grow deeper. In 1886, Gilbert sold his portion of the business to Whiting and started his own mill.

For the first time, the thirty-six-year-old Whiting now had his own paper mill. By 1888, the mill was thriving. Whiting had approximately seventy-five employees and was producing seven tons of high-grade book paper and colored writing paper each day, all on one small seventy-six-inch trim, Fourdrinier paper machine and other machinery necessary for the manufacture of rag-content paper.

On the night of August 23, 1888, disaster struck the mill. As the tragedy made its way around the country, this is how the *New York Times* chronicled the scene:

> *NEENAH, Wis., Aug. 23. — At 12 o'clock last night the large paper mill owned by George Whiting, situated on the island between this city and Menasha, was destroyed by fire. While the burning structure was surrounded by a crowd of spectators the battery of boilers exploded. The roof and the walls were thrown outward, sending a shower of bricks and timbers among the spectators. Eighteen persons were killed, seven severely injured, and a number less seriously hurt.*
>
> *The mill was a three-story structure, built four years ago at a cost of $100,000, and was operated day and night. When the flames broke out about 50 men were in the building. The fire alarm brought several hundred people to the spot, who crowded as close to the burning building as the intense heat would permit. About 1:30 o'clock, while the building was a mass of flames, the explosion occurred without warning. The roof of the building was thrown upward and outward, the walls of brick crumbled and crashed into the street, and in an instant scores of men were buried*

Left: Employees at George A. Whiting Paper Mill posing next to paper machine, circa 1890. *Courtesy of the Whiting family private collection.*

Below: Employees posing outside of George A. Whiting Paper Mill, circa 1905. *Courtesy of the Whiting family private collection.*

> *by the heavy debris. There was a moment of silence and then a cry of horror went up from the multitude. The first strong impulse to fly from possible further danger was soon overcome, and hundreds began the work of recovering the bodies of the dead and rescuing and caring for the injured. Body after body was found, crushed and mangled by the great timbers and masonry almost beyond recognition, and then removed to the City Hall. The injured were carried to neighboring residences or to their homes as soon as their identity could be established…*
>
> *A number of men, women, and boys were also injured by being hit by missiles from the explosion, but none except those whose names are mentioned are seriously wounded. All of the killed will be buried at the city's expense, as they are all in poor circumstances, and some of the families of the killed are almost destitute. Mayor Lawson had appointed a committee to solicit aid for the families of the killed, and already a good deal of money has been subscribed.*
>
> *Every factory in the city is closed to-day and will remain so until after the burials. Flags are at half mast on all the public buildings. The City Council held a meeting to-night for the purpose of taking action in regard to the funerals, which will probably occur Sunday.*

The paper also listed the names of those killed and seriously wounded. About $3,000 was raised by the town to assist grieving families, equivalent to about $75,000 today. One-third of the money was donated by Charles B. Clark.

George Whiting was devastated but rebuilt. Again, the mill thrived. By 1891, Whiting was expanding to the Wisconsin River region, pioneering papermaking there by opening mills in Plover and eventually Stevens Point.

When George A. Whiting died in 1930, his legacy as a paper pioneer was firmly planted throughout Wisconsin. His son, Frank Whiting, assumed control of the company and the Menasha mill, as did every generation after him, with the company remaining family-owned throughout virtually its entire existence.

Whiting Paper evolved over time to remain competitive in a global market. It catered to a specialized market of custom papers, utilized the same paper machine for its first 104 years in business, and was able to increase capacity from internal growth, rejecting the notion of being purchased by a larger company with greater capital.

But by the early 2000s, the small mill had evolved all it could. When the final order was shipped from the George A. Whiting Paper Company in Menasha in 2016, it was one of the oldest and smallest paper mills in

Remains of George A. Whiting Paper Mill, erected in 1882. *Courtesy of Scott Wittman Visual, 2018.*

the largest paper milling state, unable any longer to weather the changing twenty-first-century times.

George Whiting's old partner, William Markley Gilbert, went on to have an illustrious career as well—along with his father and three brothers. The Gilberts built a paper mill along the new Lawson Canal in Menasha in 1887. The mill also had an envelope factory attached, employing, at opening, close to two hundred people. Throughout its history, the Gilbert Paper Company produced high-quality cotton fiber content papers, a combination of wood and cotton, including bond, ledger, index and onionskin papers. The process is still used universally today. Gilbert was also nationally recognized as producing the finest writing papers, for which the popularity of the typewriter boosted demand and production. To attain such paper grades, the mill used waters drilled from artesian wells, according to the *Appleton Post*, "The only factory of its kind west of Massachusetts."

Within a year, eight more factories were erected along the Lawson Canal, cut specifically for waterpower, adding an economic boom for the city of Menasha.

By 1922, Gilbert Paper was pushing twenty tons of paper a day along with printing currency for Russia, China, Brazil, Mexico, Argentina and the

Employees at Gilbert Paper Company, circa 1900. *Courtesy of the Paper Discovery Center.*

United States of America. It was now the second-largest paper mill in the Neenah-Menasha area, behind only the giant Kimberly-Clark.

As with the Whiting Mill, Gilbert Paper was also a family affair, with each generation taking over for the last, until the mill was sold to the Mead Corporation in 1960 for financial stability. For several more decades to follow, Gilbert continued to provide stability for hundreds of employees and their families, until profits began drying up. Fox River Paper Company eventually obtained the facility in 2001 and moved operations to other facilities. The mill closed in 2003.

The wrecking ball arrived in April 2008, taking down the massive structure that had numerous additions erected through the years and had grown to over 250,000 square feet, exposing a view of the Fox River not seen for well over a century. The Gilbert office building, built in 1919, remains standing today. The two-story, redbrick Georgian Revival now houses a law firm and is the sole remnant of a paper mill that dominated the scene along Ahnaip Street in Menasha for 122 years.

Just off the corner of Wisconsin Avenue and Church Street in downtown Neenah, on the southern banks of where the Fox River widens into Little

Gilbert Paper Mill, 1960. *Courtesy of the Paper Discovery Center.*

Lake Butte des Morts, lies a street-side park. The park contains a large stone arch that greets visitors as they walk along a paved path to a smooth, redbrick, triangular wall with massive stone trim, as well as a truncated smokestack, which is the central figure. These are the remnants of the Bergstrom Paper Mill office building, a Romanesque Revival structure built in 1893, and once was accompanied by a twenty-five-structure paper mill complex.

Legacy Park pays homage to the papermaking history of the area, with plaques showcased around the smokestack recognizing the contributions of the pioneers of the local industry. Privately financed, Legacy Park stands as a memorial and tribute to those who helped build the Fox Cities community. The park stands on the site where the Winnebago Paper Mill, the same Winnebago Paper Mill that George Whiting eventually bought in to, was built in 1874.

John R. Davis, a Welsh immigrant, constructed the mill on the site of a burned down government-run flour mill utilized for the benefit of the Menominee Indians, who had been relocated here in 1831—even before the Treaty of the Cedars. The Winnebago Mill, like most mills in the area at the time, showed a profit almost immediately, turning out six tons a day after operations were up and running smoothly. When Whiting came on board in 1875, began overseeing floor operations in 1876 and added book paper in 1878, the Winnebago Mill was one of the most successful of the early Fox Cities papermakers.

After Whiting left to begin his own venture with Gilbert in 1882, the Winnebago began a slow, steady decline. John Davis died in 1885, and his sons turned their attention to their more prosperous mills in Eau Claire, selling the Winnebago Paper Mill to Dedric Waldemar Bergstrom in 1904.

D.W. Bergstrom arrived in America as a child, emigrating from the Netherlands with his family as a five-year-old. He and his brother, George Bergstrom, were partners, along with Havilah Babcock of Kimberly-Clark, in Bergstrom Stove Company, a successful manufacturer of stoves, furnaces and plows. Eventually, George would buy the other two out when D.W. went on to purchase the Winnebago Mill, which he gave a virtual teardown and rebuild. The 1893 office building was doubled in size during the renovation of the mill.

With his eldest son, John N. Bergstrom, as manager, and his other three sons, Willis, D.W. II and Nathan Bergstrom all on board, the Bergstrom Paper Company thrived, producing high-quality book papers. Bergstrom was also one of the first paper manufacturers to realize the environmental benefits of recycled paper, as wastepaper fibers were combined with wood pulp, creating a smooth high-grade finish that was becoming extremely desirable to customers. Bergstrom went on to become one of the leading producers of recycled paper in the world.

Over time, the Bergstrom mill was expanded throughout a full seven acres, building new warehouses, power plants, finishing rooms, a waste disposal plant, hydrapulper additions, laboratories and more paper machines, until the entire complex was a twenty-six-structure monstrosity.

In 1979, after seventy-five years of operating the paper mill, the Bergstrom family sold the mill to Glatfelter, a global manufacturer of specialty paper products based in York, Pennsylvania. In 2006, Glatfelter purchased a division of NewPage Corporation in Fremont, Ohio, as part of an $80 million transaction, transferring operations and leading to the closing of the former Bergstrom mill, creating a seven-acre-wide fracture in downtown Neenah.

In Nicholas A. Basbanes's 2014 book, *On Paper: The Everything of Its Two-Thousand-Year History,* George Glatfelter talked with Basbanes about the Neenah closing: "You learn a few things after 144 years of being in business and certain things are indelible. You might change the products you make, and you might change the market you serve; you might even change the people—that's an evolutionary process. But you don't change the value system. That's what you preserve."

After displaying for the world exactly what Glatfelter valued, the City of Neenah received state and federal grants and local government liability relief for the cleanup of the contaminated grounds and the ultimate demolition of the massive mill complex, including the 1893 office building, built by esteemed architect William Waters, which was in the National Register of Historic Places.

Not to be left out of the paper boom of the Fox Valley was Kaukauna, the site of the steepest drop of the river and the setting for two more giants to enter in to the industry. By 1870, the river at the Grand Kakalin had been harnessed to power several flour mills and sawmills, which did not go unnoticed by ambitious newcomers to the growing community. In 1872, a New York–born Civil War veteran and former Secret Service agent, Colonel Henry Frambach, along with his brother, John Stovekin, moved to Kaukauna and built the Eagle Mill. The Eagle Mill was unique, as

Bergstrom Paper Mill Office Building. Designed by William Waters in 1893, the building was razed in 2009. *Courtesy of the Wisconsin Historical Society SHPO.*

Badger Paper Mill, Kaukauna, circa 1890. *Library of Congress.*

Stovekin ran a flour mill out of the front of the building and Frambach a paper mill out of the back.

Frambach was a true eccentric. Seemingly easily bored in his escapades, he built another paper mill in Menasha in 1878, only to return his attention to the Eagle Mill in 1880, soon before the mill was destroyed by fire. After rebuilding the mill and renaming it the Frambach Paper Mill, he again set his sights on something bigger and better and sold his mill.

By 1885, there were now seven paper or pulp mills in Kaukauna. Frambach, however, was not finished. After founding the First National Bank of Kaukauna, becoming the town's first mayor and running for the U.S. House of Representatives, he built the Badger Paper Mill, a three-story behemoth facility for its day and the small town it was located in, in 1885. The mill, which also contained a sulfite plant for the production of wood pulp, was turning out twenty tons of paper and fifteen tons of sulfite every day.

In July 1897, stored paper stock spontaneously combusted in a room on the third floor of the Badger Mill. Before the fire department arrived, the flames had ripped through the roof and had already begun engulfing the rest of the building. Within just a few minutes, the mill and the sulfite plant, a wooden structure adjacent to the main limestone plant, were gone. The August 3, 1897 edition of the *Paper Mill and Wood Pulp News* chronicled the carnage:

> *Although more than a week has passed, Kaukauna has not recovered from the effects of the burning of the Badger Mill. All that remains of the extensive plant, with the exception of the boiler house and finishing department, which was but slightly damaged, is a pile of twisted, cracked, bent and ruined machinery, shafting, piping and stock, heaped between cracked, gloomy and smoke-begrimed walls. Ten days ago it was the pride of the Badger Paper Company and Kaukauna as well, but now it is a skeleton cooling off for the benefit of the insurance adjusters.*

It was time for Frambach to again try his luck elsewhere. Legal disputes with the Kaukauna Water Power Company delayed the potential process of a rebuild and the remains of the mill were leveled. Some 125 jobs were

Badger Paper Mill, Kaukauna, circa 1887. Burned in 1897. *Courtesy of the Kaukauna Public Library.*

lost, quite a number in 1897. Frambach left the Fox Cities and continued his successes in Michigan. The Kaukauna City Power Plant was built on the old mill's ashes in 1907. Today, the site houses the Kaukauna Utilities Badger Hydro Project at 777 Island Street.

Kaukauna, however, was still enjoying a growth spurt due to the paper industry. At one point after the turn of the century, as many as twelve pulp or paper mills were conducting operations along this small stretch of the Fox River, and the *Kaukauna Times* in 1890 was thrilled:

> *A regular building boom has struck Kaukauna this spring. Four brick blocks, and thirty-five residences are now in the course of construction about the city, with many more to follow.*
>
> *Day by day, Kaukauna grows, and healthy growth it is. Look to the East, look to the West, the South, or the North and the rising peak of some new building meets the eye. Step-by-step the city expands its circle, and where lofty trees rose in all their splendor 10 years ago comfortable cottages or large residence now stand, happy home of some family who has come among us, who came a few years ago with barely enough capital to get here and have by the many opportunities presented succeeded in building a place that they can call home—their home.*

Another of those who came to Kaukauna was a quiet, reserved, German immigrant named Oscar Thilmany, who invested with five partners in a small pulp and paper mill along the Fox River and wound up building a paper conglomerate in the shadows of the Grignon Mansion.

In 1883, Thilmany and five others in Kaukauna founded the American Pulp and Paper Company, of which Thilmany quickly took hold of the daily operations. In its infancy, the company had a hard time getting its feet on the ground and did little to distinguish itself from the other paper mills in Kaukauna, much less the Fox Valley in general. Additions were made to increase capacity, though little changes were noted in results.

Then in 1889, Oscar Thilmany had enough of the stagnant partnership and bought out all of the others, becoming the sole owner and changing the name to Thilmany Pulp and Paper Mill. He immediately invested in the company's first paper machine, expanded its capacity to output a variety of different papers and increased its target market and customer base. Thilmany was soon challenging Frambach's Badger Mill for superiority in Kaukauna, having been awarded the contract for printing Montgomery

Thilmany Paper Mill, circa 1900. *Courtesy of the Kaukauna Public Library.*

Thilmany Paper Mill, view from the canal, circa 1902. *Courtesy of the Paper Discovery Center.*

Ward catalogues in 1901, the largest contract awarded in the market and sought after by every papermaker in the country.

Later in 1901, Oscar Thilmany did what many today would see as the unthinkable. With the mill's future prospects soaring, Thilmany stepped aside. He sold his stock in the company to his favorite customer, California businessman Monroe A. Wertheimer, and stayed on as company president, only to relinquish that title a year later and move back to his native Germany. His reasons for leaving a flourishing business that he developed are unknown to this day. In *"A Little Ways Ahead": The Centennial History of Thilmany Pulp and Paper Company*, authors William Bremer and Holly Lyon write,

> *Nobody knows today what Oscar Thilmany was thinking during the time that he lived and worked in Kaukauna, Wisconsin. He never wrote his reminiscences, and people who know him did not record their recollections of what he thought. Nonetheless, the pattern of his actions suggests that Thilmany was a determined man who would have viewed his opportunities with calm assurance.*

Office in Thilmany Paper Mill. Calendar indicates April 1902, mere months before Oscar Thilmany left the mill to move back to his native Germany. *Courtesy of the Paper Discovery Center.*

The company started by Oscar Thilmany is the only operating paper company that survives in Kaukauna to this day.

The Eagle Mill, the first paper mill ever built in Kaukauna, today remains as the only representative structure of the late nineteenth-century papermaking boom in the city. After changing hands several times throughout the decades, the Eagle Mill was purchased by the neighboring Thilmany Pulp and Paper Mill in 1941, with both campuses combined into one, the buildings connected with a large, single-story office addition and a second-story skywalk. The complex was being added to as recently as the 1980s, until Thilmany, now operated by Finnish-owned Ahlstrom-Munksjo, moved all of its operations to a more modern facility adjacent—and closed the Eagle Mill and original Thilmany complex in 2012. During renovations of the area in 2013, all later additions to the original Eagle Mill building and the Thilmany complex were demolished, leaving the 1881 Eagle Mill standing in Kaukauna and now housing the city's public library.

Throughout the twentieth century, papermaking in the Fox Cities continued to prosper. The original generation of industry pioneers gave way to their successors who seamlessly carried out their original visions, weaving through economic depressions, recessions and labor unrest while advancing the daily conveniences and communicative habits of the world's population.

The leader of the papermaking trade and commercial enterprise continued to be Kimberly-Clark, both in the Fox Cities and nationally. K-C mills in Neenah, Appleton, Kimberly and De Pere flourished, and further expansion was imminent. Kimberly-Clark's research and development laboratory in Neenah was the birthplace of personal hygiene tissue paper products, sold under such names as Kleenex, Kotex and Huggies, which would eventually rebrand the entire company.

Signs of that rebrand, and an omen for things to come, unseen at the time, occurred on 1976, when Kimberly-Clark began to sell off its commodity paper mills to focus exclusively on the personal hygiene products market, and apparently no mill was off-limits.

For eighty-seven years, the Kimberly Mill supported its namesake town, and the town likewise rallied around the mill, drawing its identity and blue-collar, middle-class pride from the shift-work and toil spent to keep the mill—and the town—afloat.

Not much was made of the sale at the time, as the mill was purchased by the Repap Corporation with little inconvenience to employees or the town. But then, in 1997 it was sold to Consolidated Papers and then again in 2000 to Stora Enso, when departments began to be merged and lower

Thilmany employees sitting on pile of rags to be processed into paper, 1902. *Courtesy of the Paper Discovery Center.*

Two employees posing in 1902 at Thilmany Mill. *Courtesy of the Paper Discovery Center.*

Kimberly-Clark Kimberly Mill, circa 1910. Razed in 2011. *Courtesy of the Winnebago County Historical and Archaeological Society.*

Kimberly Mill employees, circa 1910. *Courtesy of the Kimberly Public Library.*

tenured workers eliminated. In 2007, the mill was sold to NewPage, the same corporation that had sold a division of its business to Glatfelter in 2006, leading to the closure of the former Bergstrom Paper Mill in Neenah just a year earlier. People now began to pay attention.

Ultimately, it was announced in 2008 that the Kimberly Mill would close. NewPage, with the mill being in perfect working order with modern updates and a desirable workforce, received several offers of purchase from potential buyers to keep the mill running. Refusing to sell to a competitor, NewPage elected to cripple a town; six hundred people, in a community of six thousand, were out of work, the lowest time served by any individual employee being twenty-eight years. Demolition was done in phases and began in 2011, continuing for several years. The site is now a residential community. Every July, in Sunset Park on the banks of the Fox River, Kimberly continues to host Paperfest, a summer festival celebrating the area's papermaking heritage, as it has for decades. "Now that the Kimberly Mill has closed," reads the event's website, "this name is a reminder of the community history we came from and the future we share." Kimberly's high school teams and students continue with their moniker, the Papermakers.

The twenty-first century has been a time of change and evolution for the Fox Cities' paper industry. Fifteen years after Kimberly-Clark's relocation of its headquarters from Neenah to Texas in 1984, the Atlas Mill in Appleton went dark. Five years after that, the Institute of Paper Chemistry moved from the campus of Lawrence University to the campus of Georgia Tech.

The freefall was on.

The state of Wisconsin lost more than one-third of its paper mill jobs between 2005 and 2015, the brunt of that pain felt in the Fox River Valley. The hits seemingly just kept coming upon the community, as Kimberly-Clark announced in 2018 that it was cutting 12–13 percent of its entire global workforce, including two plants in the Fox Cities. The harsh, personal realities of plant closings such as these was depicted in an Associated Press article when the closing of the Gilbert Paper Mill in Menasha was announced in 2001:

> *Tom Strebe is a third-generation worker at the Gilbert Paper Co. mill. Now he and his wife, Rhonda, another Gilbert veteran, face the prospect of losing their entire livelihood with the expected closing of the plant at the end of November.*

"We both have insurance there, and we have three kids. Now we're done. It's scary," Rhonda Strebe said hours after hearing the news this week of the impending shutdown.

She has 13 years' experience at Gilbert. Her husband is a 14-year veteran at the plant. They learned Monday of the deal that is expected to shut down a mill that has operated for 114 years.

Fox River Paper Co. of Appleton plans to acquire the business and selected assets of Gilbert. Mead Corp., Gilbert's parent company, intends to close the mill once the transaction is concluded, which is expected to be Nov. 30.

Fox River will continue operating Gilbert's converting mill in Greenville. About 100 current employees out of the 270 at Gilbert will join Fox River, but the rest will be out of a job.

The news came a month after Mead, of Dayton, Ohio, and Westvaco Corp., of Stamford, Conn., announced their intention to merge, creating a new $8 billion organization called MeadWestvaco Corp.

Company officials said at the time that various facilities would be reviewed over the next year for possible streamlining of operations.

Gilbert employees said they received telephone calls from the company Sunday, saying they shouldn't report for work Monday and instead should attend an informational meeting at a Neenah hotel.

Retiree Gary Mortenson, a veteran of 39 years at Gilbert and maintenance superintendent before he left the company nine years ago, said he was not surprised to hear of the planned shutdown.

"I was not really shocked to hear it. I expected it, the way the economy is and the way they've been running," he said. "Their orders have been way down."

Company officials said they could not discuss how hourly employees will be affected until meeting with officials from Local 1477 of the Paper, Allied-Industrial, Chemical & Energy International Union (PACE).

The company said salaried workers would receive a severance offering based on their years of service and annual compensation. Strebe, 42, a mill supervisor, said he and his wife are sizing up their options with their children, ages 10 to 17. They may move to North Carolina to be nearer Rhonda Strebe's family.

"We'll figure out something," Tom Strebe said. "So much for corporate America, huh?"

Women working at Fox River Paper Company when the men were overseas during World War II, circa 1945. Photo depicts very early usage of fluorescent lights. *Courtesy of the Paper Discover Center.*

When walking at Legacy Park in Neenah, among the Romanesque-style limestone remnants and bronze plaques commemorating the paper pioneers of the Fox Cities, on the site that supported paper mill workers and their families for 132 years, a redbrick, tree-lined, paved path leads into the rest of the redeveloped site. The path points the way to the global headquarters of

Legacy Park on the grounds of the former Bergstrom Paper Mill. *Courtesy of Scott Wittman Visual, 2018.*

Plexus Corporation, a designer and manufacturer of electronic components, built here in 2009.

The scene is one of surreal irony. The digital revolution, along with cheaper paper from global markets, has been mostly responsible for the decline of the paper industry and the ultimate loss of a lifestyle. On this spot, where an electronics manufacturer casts its shadow over land wrought by the hands of the papermaker, a community's past and future are displayed in the present, much like 135 years ago, when Henry Frambach and Oscar Thilmany built their dreams on an island in the Grand Kakalin, under the watchful eye of the Charles A. Grignon Mansion.

In 1947, a contingent of residents in Plover, a small community on the Wisconsin River in central Wisconsin, held a special vote to break away from Plover and incorporate their own village, due to some perceived municipal shortcomings afforded them by the city. The vote passed overwhelmingly, and a name was now needed for the newly incorporated community.

They voted to name the community after a local industrial pioneer and organizer of several paper mills in the area that were the lifeblood of the local population, a pioneer who created an identity and a way of life in the community that supported employees, their families and past and future generations.

They voted to name their village Whiting.

STEAMBOATS AND WATERPOWER

On June 16, 1856, the shores of the lower Fox River were overrun with people. Music was playing, flags and banners were waving, and cheering commenced as the whole of the Fox Cities crowded into the streets leading down to the riverbanks. The people had all turned out to see what was later recorded as "one of the most beautiful sights we have ever seen."

There, *Pioneer*, a steamboat from Green Bay, had just left the southernmost lock in Appleton. As it glided into the Fox River headed toward Menasha, around the bend and into the basin came another steamboat, the *Aquila*, going in the opposite direction.

The crowd erupted into cheer. The *Aquila* had become the first steamer to ever navigate the new Fox-Wisconsin waterway, a system of strategically placed locks, dams and canals linking the Mississippi River with the Great Lakes, a monumental national event at the time, with the Fox Cities being front and center.

Both steamers stopped in the Fox River at Appleton and exchanged greetings in a "marriage of the waters." Steam whistles filled the air, increasing the roar of the crowd. Brass bands from Appleton, Neenah and Menasha boarded the *Aquila* and rode with it to Green Bay. A contingent of officials from all the Fox Cities boarded as well, giving speeches at commencement ceremonies later in the evening.

When the steamer reached Green Bay, the festivities grew more robust, with the *Appleton Crescent* describing, "Every vessel in the harbor crowded

Thistle at unidentified dock, circa 1906. *Courtesy of the Neenah Public Library.*

with people, every warehouse, dock, lumber pile, and riverbank loaded with yelling people. The streets leading to the river were a mass of noisy humanity." Guns and cannons at Fort Howard greeted the steamer, parades formed and a dinner and dance on the steamboat *Sultana* finally capped the night.

The side-wheel steamer *Isabell* at Oshkosh, circa 1880. Built in 1871, the boat was "dismantled" in 1897. *Courtesy of the Kaukauna Public Library.*

The *Aquila* had set sail in Pittsburgh and traveled down the Ohio River, to the Mississippi, up through the Wisconsin River, through the Portage Canal and government canal in Menasha, into Appleton and finally north to Green Bay and into Lake Michigan, opening a shipping route for goods and passengers to and from the Fox Cities.

A commercial boom had commenced, and an era wrought with the romanticism of riverboats and weekend excursions was about to begin its short life.

The opening of the lower Fox River to boat traffic and linking the Fox to the Mississippi River had been bandied about for two centuries before anyone took a practical approach to completing such an undertaking. The upper Fox, west of Oshkosh, was basically a slow, meandering stream that could be dredged enough to pass, but the lower Fox was raging, as evidenced by the names given to local towns, such as Grand Chute, Little Chute and Grand Kakalin. Canals needed to be dug, dams needed to be built and locks created for boats to maneuver the falling waters.

For thirty years, beginning in the 1840s, numerous attempts at improving the waterway for commercial ventures were made. A few dams and locks were built, but by 1872, painfully slow progress had been made. After financial failures of multiple private undertakings, the Army Corps of Engineers

Steamboat traffic jam in Lake Winnebago in Neenah, circa 1910. *Courtesy of the Neenah Public Library.*

stepped in, purchased the entire waterway and completed the process. Due to the massive increase in industrial production occurring on the river in the Fox Valley at the time, it became imperative to be completed in a timely manner. By 1884, the riverway was improved enough to provide free water routes for travel and commerce—as tolls were initially charged—as well as for purposes of national defense, which is one reason the U.S. government was so keen on taking the project over. The waterway was open, and the steamboat era on the Fox River had begun.

Many of the steamboats in operation on the Fox were locally built, usually in Oshkosh by the Ryan Brothers Shipbuilding Company, utilizing the abundant resources of native pine and oak. The U.S. Army Corps of Engineers eventually standardized the locks, which had sometimes stretched over 165 feet long, to 145 feet, thus keeping the length of the steamers in check.

One of the oldest and most popular of the passenger steamboats of the day was the *Evelyn*, a 125-foot-long stern-wheeler built in Oshkosh in 1883. Its two-hundred-horsepower engine was able to carry five hundred people with a seven-man crew and paraded the waters between Oshkosh and Green Bay for passenger excursions for twenty-five years.

In an ad posted in the *Appleton Evening Crescent* on July 30, 1904, the *Evelyn* was commissioned by the Outagamie County Sunday School Association to provide transportation for a picnic in Neenah. An appropriate illustration of the steamboat lifestyle reads as follows:

> *Steamboats "Evelyn" and "Carter" will leave the Government dock at Appleton at 9 a.m. sharp and arrive at the park about 10:30. The "Evelyn" and "Carter" are the two safest boats on the river. Care will be taken that they are not overloaded.*
>
> *At the park an elaborate program of field sports will be given—footraces, potato races, sack races, wrestling matches, and a baseball game. The steamboats will make one-hour trips from the park on Lake Winnebago during the day at 10 cents a trip.*

Such events were common during the days of the riverboats. Area newspapers routinely ran advertisements announcing various excursions, telling readers the time and place of the boat's departure and how to return. Riverboats have also lived longer in the memory of the modern-day Fox River Valley than anything else from its past days. Nothing invokes more of the romantic and poetic side of the river than the stories of the *Evelyn, Thistle, Mayflower, Isabell, Leander Choate* or *Valley Queen*. Steamboats were often the chosen setting for social activities, such as dances and picnic excursions, which would've been sponsored by local churches, schools or various civic groups.

In 1907, after almost a quarter century of sailing through the locks of the Fox, the *Evelyn* was condemned by government inspectors as being unsafe for excursions and its permit was revoked. It was noted its hull was no longer in condition to allow for heavy passenger traffic. Regulations on such began to tighten around the time due to several disasters on steamboats due to overages of capacity and faulty safety equipment, mainly on the East Coast, spelling the end for many of the older steamers. The *Evelyn* spent its remaining days on the water hauling coal and general merchandise between the Fox Cities and Green Bay, for which the permit revocation did not matter.

Later that year, a local farmer noticed the remains of an abandoned beached boat on land he owned off the shore of Lake Butte des Morts. The boiler and engines had been removed, leaving a large wooden shell. Attempting to pry the skeleton free from the mud, the farmer was unable,

Leander Choate on a Fox River excursion, circa 1910. *Courtesy of the Menasha Public Library.*

Passengers aboard the *Leander Choate* waiting to depart, circa 1911. *Courtesy of the Neenah Public Library.*

choosing instead to cut it to pieces and use it for firewood. And so, there ended the life of the once grand *Evelyn*.

Whoever beached the *Evelyn*, however, kept its boiler and engines because they were placed in a new steamer, the *Leander Choate II*, named after a prominent local entrepreneur and founder of the Oshkosh Grass Matting Company. The first steamboat of that name was built in 1884, though it burned in 1885.

Also built by the Ryan Shipbuilding Company of Oshkosh in 1908 and first sailing in 1910, the *Leander Choate* was dimensionally large, pushing the maximum capacity suggested by the Corps, and at 145 feet long able to carry 550 passengers. Each year, from early May through September, the stern-wheeler could be seen on excursions up and down the river, an iconic sight of summer in the turn-of-the-century Fox Valley.

In 1921, the *Leander Choate* was sold and extensively remodeled, its upper deck transformed into a large dance floor. Its new owners renamed the boat the *Valley Queen*. After only two seasons with its new identity, the steamer caught fire while at dock in Oshkosh in November 1922, ending the *Valley Queen*'s excursion days forever. Just a month later, an article in the *Appleton Evening Crescent* read like a eulogy to an already bygone era:

The *K.M. Hutchinson* stern-wheeler in the Menasha canal, circa 1890. Built in Oshkosh in 1886, it burned on a sandbar in Winneconne in 1895. *Courtesy of Neenah Public Library.*

The *Mayflower Jr.* stern-wheel steamer at Kaukauna, 1914. Built in Oshkosh in 1913, the boat passes out of documentation by 1940. *Courtesy of the Kaukauna Public Library.*

No Big Pleasure Steamers Left to Ply on Waters Here

Although navigation is still open, Appleton drawbridges are being opened with comparative infrequency and then only to admit coal barges. Large pleasure boats are in unknown quantity on the river these days. With the recent burning of the Valley Queen, *that made many excursion trips to Appleton this summer, the last large excursion steamer has been removed.*

The Paul L. *was dismantled recently, having outlived her usefulness, and some of her machinery was transferred to the* Mayflower, *a smaller boat. It is only a few years back when the* Evelyn, *the* Thistle, *the* Paul L *and the* Leander Choate *plied up the river. But now they are all gone, probably due to the extensive use of the automobile as a pleasure vehicle.*

To be fair to the automobile, the railroad was just as much to blame for the short life of the steamboat, although both proved deadly to the era. By the time the *Aquila* made its maiden voyage through the Fox-Wisconsin waterway into the Fox Cities in 1856, the railroads were already being built. The days of the river being essential for travel were already approaching an end.

And as for the fate of the *Aquila*? A year after making its famous passage from Pittsburgh, it ran into troubled waters in Lake Winnebago and sank in ten feet of water before it could make it to shore. The steamer was raised, but eventually abandoned. Its machinery was used in the building of a new riverboat, the *Ellwood*.

Such was the typical end to the romantic steamboats of the Fox River. Most were dismantled and burned or sunk when no longer needed. Some were turned into barges to haul coal, wood pulp and other various commercial goods, and some were sold off and never heard from again. The *Paul L* is still lying underneath the waters of the Fox River in downtown Appleton, under the Lawe Street Bridge.

A few of the earlier riverboats went on to have more exciting, albeit tragic, careers. The aforementioned *Ellwood*, after once missing Lock No. 4 in Appleton and falling broadside over the dam, killing two of its crew, was sold and became a floating hospital on the Mississippi River during the Civil War. The *Appleton Belle* somehow got into Confederate hands, though it was recaptured by the Union and burned in the Ohio River.

After the demise of the steamboats, the barges and tugboats had the river all to themselves. Not nearly as glamorous or romantic in reminiscence, their job was a necessity for the burgeoning industrial growth of the region. The barges fed the industries, hauling coal, lumber and pulp to be utilized for power or raw materials. The railroads did not affect the barges because the barges were basically supplementing the railroads, as the trains themselves couldn't keep up with the rapid turnaround of the seemingly endless paper and pulp mills lining the river.

The barges were not attractive, as many were black with coal and soot, but their whistles sounding became a routine part of the life of anyone who lived around the river, as the barges were operating twenty-four hours a day, not unlike what we hear with today's railroad horns.

The barges of the Fox River Navigation Company and the Cook & Brown Lime Company, the two enterprises handling the barge traffic, also had short life spans. This time it wasn't the railroads that were to blame, it was natural gas, which was profoundly cheaper to use for fuel, along with the advent of over-the-road trucking and vast improvements to roads and the highway system. By 1959, the barges followed their predecessor steamboats into Fox River history.

Coal barge in ice on Fox River, view looking east from the Kimberly-Little Chute bridge, circa 1950. *Courtesy of the Andrew J. Mueller Collection at the History Museum at the Castle.*

Coal barge clearing Lock No. 1 in Appleton, circa 1945. *Courtesy of the Andrew J. Mueller Collection at the History Museum at the Castle.*

Leisure recreation on the Cedars Lock between Little Chute and Kimberly, circa 1950. Abandonment left this lock with considerable water leakage resulting in significant deterioration, which has since been restored. *Courtesy of the Andrew J. Mueller Collection at the History Museum at the Castle.*

Kaukauna Lock No. 2 near Thilmany Mill, circa 1920s. Abandonment caused mortar displacement, rotting wood and general disrepair. Since restored. *Courtesy of the Kaukauna Public Library.*

By 1982, although recreational boaters continued to utilize the seventeen locks along the Fox River from Neenah to De Pere, the U.S. Army Corps of Engineers, which still owned the locks from when it took over the waterway in 1872 said the locks were "low priority." Commercial traffic on the river was virtually absent for twenty years, which was long enough for the Corps to wait. The expenditure of federal dollars on such a low-usage waterway would not be supported. It was announced that the navigational season would close a month early that year, in October, and would no longer reopen in the spring. The locks were to be closed for operation and placed into "caretaker" status, meaning the Corps of Engineers would simply maintain the locks for flood control, though they would no longer be operational. The dams would continue to be regulated.

The locks, some of which by this point were 130 years old and in massive need of repair, were abandoned. Not only were no federal dollars spent, but the Corps of Engineers also floated filling them in and dismantling them completely, virtually closing the Fox River in the Fox Cities to travel forever.

For a quarter century, local municipalities debated what to do about the abandoned locks, as state taxpayer money was not going to be allocated to save a system that many taxpayers wouldn't utilize. Meanwhile, the condition of the locks worsened.

The cut stone masonry walls were bowed in toward the center of the locks. Water was leaking in the stone mortar joints, in both the walls and the gates, causing extensive displacement of mortar, weakening the joints to the point that some joints were void of mortar completely. Heavy vegetation was growing over lock walls and gates, clogging canals.

Also falling into disrepair were the lock tender houses, which sat adjacent to the locks and were the residences of the lockmasters and their families in order to provide twenty-four-hour response to boat traffic. Each lock had to be opened by hand-turning a crank around a set of gears that slowly opened the lock doors.

The lock tenders themselves became fairly prominent men in the community, as their retirements, often after decades on the job, were routinely announced in the newspapers of the day.

John Vander Linden had been a lock tender for only four days when the *Ellwood* went over the dam, killing two crew members. He retired thirty-four years later, when the government moved his lockhouse across the canal from the Atlas Mill, where his wife would be unable to cross, as she was in a wheelchair.

Lock tenders on Appleton Lock No. 3, circa 1900. *Courtesy of the Neenah Historical Society.*

George T. Allanson retired from the Menasha lock in 1932 after forty-five years. His father ran the locks there for eight years prior, marking fifty-three years during which a lock was tendered by the same family.

The job of a lock tender was often dangerous and harrowing. These men were charged with ensuring safe travel through the river, raging with current and dams and power, of vessels carrying cargos of both humans and goods. Oftentimes, they were credited with saving others from drowning, and some drowned themselves. Injuries were frequent, as losing one's footing while turning the large hand-cranks was not uncommon, resulting in large gashes and head wounds. The reputation of a lock tender was one of honor and service, sometimes even to the point of exaggeration.

One of these men was Mike Kirby, who, it was reported by the *Post-Crescent* at the time of his death in 1911, was "familiarly known by every man, woman and child in Appleton for about a quarter-century" and had a reputation as being the best fighter in the Fox River Valley. Kirby was the lock tender at Lock No. 1 in Appleton and has the distinction of being the first lock tender ever in Appleton and the second on the river, as Menasha was the first lock built. One day, after Kirby had retired from the locks, he was coming into Appleton on his wagon when he was apparently struck by a

Northwestern train. "The wagon was reduced to splinters," it was reported, "and Mr. Kirby was thrown 50 feet from the track, but escaped with only a few scratches and bruises, not a bone being broken."

For almost thirty years, the houses of the lock tenders and their families sat vacant, a victim of government red tape and politics. Their stories faded into the distance. Their houses faded into decay. And the locks they sat alongside crumbled. In 2004, the State of Wisconsin did procure the right to purchase the locks back from the federal government and created the Fox River Navigational System Authority to oversee the restoration of the locks for recreational use as well as the lock tender houses. Today, a number of lockhouses along the Fox River stand tall once again, a tribute to the days of the lock tender and his family, another vestige of the Fox River's past living only in photographs and memory.

It was a simple bass-fishing trip in the spring of 1882 that sparked an idea—an idea formulated by a conversation between prominent entrepreneur H.J. Rogers, an executive at the Appleton Pulp and Paper Company, and his fishing buddy, H.E. Jacobs, who was employed by the Western Electric Light Company of Chicago. The conversation centered around the current construction taking place of the Pearl Street Power Station in New York, which was to become the world's first commercial central power plant utilizing the Edison system—which consisted of a central power station equipped with generators, or dynamos, voltage regulators and copper wiring connecting the generator to the Edison-invented incandescent lightbulbs inside the structure to be lit. As that plant was to be fired by steam (and then coal when steam proved unreliable), Rogers, who was in the process of building a new home in Appleton, thought about the possibilities of building a power station in Appleton, generated by the waters of the Fox River. When Rogers returned home, he joined with several other Appleton business partners and formed the Appleton Edison Light Company and began the process of making his vision a reality.

Rogers and Company took several trips to Chicago to learn about the process from leading engineers. Two Edison "K" dynamos were procured, as well as the rights to utilize the Edison system in the Fox Valley, with a strict stipulation that no commercial generation of electricity could occur until after Pearl Street Station began operations. Rumors began swirling at this time that the Appleton Edison Light Company had purchased the rights to the Edison system strictly to bury it in the Fox Valley, eliminating possible competition for its gas enterprise, but a local reporter found this to

The Hearthstone, the first home ever lit by hydroelectricity using the Edison system. *Courtesy of Scott Wittman Visual, 2018.*

be "without the slightest foundation in fact." He reported, on September 9, 1882, that the company had purchased the rights "for the purpose of giving the system a practical test, and if it proves an unquestioned success, and of course it cannot fail to, then the lights will be substituted generally for gas in all our public and private buildings....Verily this is a progressive age and Appleton keeps abreast of the times in everything tangible."

Rogers had one dynamo installed in the beater room of his Appleton Pulp and Paper Mill, directly under the bluff where he was building his new house. Both the dynamo and the pulp beater were to be run by the same waterwheel.

During construction of the home, designed by Oshkosh's William Waters, Rogers added the wiring for his new enterprise and hid the wires under insulation in the walls. The Appleton Pulp and Paper Mill was also wired, as it held the makeshift power station in its basement, as was the neighboring Vulcan Mill, owned by Kimberly-Clark.

On the afternoon of September 27, 1882, the time for the grand experiment to electrically light the three wired buildings had arrived, but initial attempts failed due to what was deemed as an excess of humidity in the paper mill. A few days later, in what the superintendent of the power

Waterpower and mills on Fox River at Appleton, circa 1880. *Courtesy of the Neenah Public Library.*

Mills along Fox River in Kaukauna, circa 1890. *Courtesy of the Neenah Public Library.*

plant later admitted was purely trial and error, "Nobody knew what would happen," the experiment failed again.

Later that same night, however, on Saturday, September 30, 1882, Appleton was "bright as day." Only twenty-six days after the Pearl Street Station lighted several buildings on Wall Street in New York City, powering Edison's incandescent lightbulbs with steam, Appleton was the first city in North America to do so with water from a central hydroelectric power station. H.J. Rogers's home, today known as the Hearthstone, was the first private residence in the world to be lit in the same manner.

About a month after this momentous occasion, the dynamo was moved outside of the Appleton Pulp and Paper Mill and into a shed attached to the building. It was also put on its own waterwheel, vastly improving its efficiency.

The second dynamo purchased by Rogers and his Appleton Edison Light Company was placed in the Vulcan Street Plant and began operation in November 1882. This building is remembered today as being the first Edison central hydroelectric power station in the world, though it more accurately should be referred to as the first freestanding Edison hydroelectric power station, as the first two were actually inside the Appleton Pulp & Paper Mill, and then in a shed attached to it. This station powered several more industrial properties and homes in Appleton and was located on Vulcan Street close to its intersection with South Island Street.

The Appleton Pulp and Paper Company mill was one of the oldest buildings in the Fox Cities when it made history. Starting as a rake factory before the Civil War, it was expanded and converted to a paper mill and soon began turning out close to fifteen tons of paper per day.

The mill's conversion to a pulp and paper facility was made in 1870, eight years before its neighbor, the Atlas, eventually was erected by Kimberly-Clark. A coffer dam extending 100 feet into the river was built, enclosing an area of river to be pumped out for placement of the mill expansion's foundation. The initial structure, added to over time, was 159 feet by 66 feet and two stories high. The machinery inside the mill's walls was powered by three massive waterwheels, grinding timber into pulp and turning that pulp to paper. By 1880, it was described by the *Appleton Post* as "one of the most prominent manufacturing establishments in Appleton, as well as one of the very largest paper mills in the west."

Nine years after the mill housed the first hydroelectric power station, it became the setting of a cruel force of irony. On August 26, 1891, while the mill had been closed for a week in order to install a modern system of automatic fire sprinklers, the mill's rag room spontaneously combusted, similar to

Parts of the still visible foundation of the former Appleton Pulp and Paper Mill, just to the west of the current Paper Discovery Center. Built in 1870, the mill was dismantled in 1908. *Courtesy of Scott Wittman Visual, 2018.*

what happened to the Badger Mill in Kaukauna six years later. Much of the mostly wood-framed building was brought down in minutes, an all-too-familiar end. The sprinkler system had been only about halfway completed.

The owners of the mill, the Van Nortwicks, did salvage part of the mill and rebuilt to at least continue some operations, but the "Little Pulp Mill," as it was thereafter referred to, was dismantled in 1908. H.J. Rogers and his family left Appleton in 1893. The foundation of his beloved paper mill can still be seen today in the shadow of the bluff atop of which his home, still containing some of the original raw copper wiring and wall switches, continues to proudly stand.

The fate of the original Vulcan Street Plant is less clear. After 1887, it disappears from maps. There is no known account of it being destroyed by fire or other means. A larger power station was built on (Olde) Oneida Street in 1886, and the two original dynamos were moved there and housed together, along with additional units. It is likely the original station was taken down soon after. An archaeological dig was conducted in the late 1970s to attempt to find the exact original location of the small, crudely built wooden station, with no success. It is surmised that the plant's timber foundations are likely located underneath five feet of fill under what is now the concrete sidewalk along the west side of Lawe Street, close to where the replica stands today.

The larger power station burned down in 1900, taking the original dynamos with it.

The Vulcan Mill, the Kimberly-Clark mill neighboring the Appleton Pulp and Paper Mill to the east and also lighted on that historic night, was dismantled along with Van Nortwick's mill in 1908 for the construction of a large powerhouse to power Kimberly-Clark's Kimberly Mill.

Just months after the big reveal on September 30, 1882, the central hydroelectric plant was supplying electricity to the Appleton Pulp and Paper Mill, Patten & Company's Paper Mill of Appleton, Valley Iron Works, Vulcan Paper Mill, Appleton Woolen Mills, Appleton Blast Furnace, Fleming's Flax Mills and the Waverly House Hotel, among numerous private residences. Of these structures, which were part of American engineering history, only the Appleton Woolen Mills remain, along with the Hearthstone and a few sporadically spread around the current Lawrence University campus. All others have been lost to time.

The Vulcan Power House, which was put in place of the Vulcan and Tioga Paper Mills, transmitted 550 kilowatts of power to the Kimberly Mill via steam and water. Its production capabilities were doubled in 1916, and it soon started providing power to the nearby Atlas Mill, though by midcentury its wooden gears and twenty-five-cycle generators became obsolete. Electing to purchase power from other providers rather than generate it itself, Kimberly-Clark halted operation of the powerhouse in 1970 and closed it for good in 1974, a victim of never-ending skyrocketing energy prices.

The building sat abandoned for years on Vulcan Island, where the Vulcan Paper Mill, Tioga Paper Mill and Appleton Pulp and Paper Mill had all sat before it, a canal separating the island from the shore. Overgrown brush, boarded-up windows and rusted scrap metal lying outside created an eyesore even for this, the industrial "flats" area of Appleton.

Work commenced on a redevelopment plan in the late 1990s, and by 2003, the canal was filled in and the building was converted into the restaurant that stands there today.

BECOMING ONE COMMUNITY

There is today a video in existence and available for viewing of Appleton in 1930. Images often have a way of articulating scenes and expressions in ways to which words simply cannot do justice, and this would be one of those examples.

The old, black-and-white film was shot from a sixteen-millimeter camera that had been mounted to the front of an electric streetcar. It's a bit of a bumpy watch, as one can imagine, as the streetcar follows its tracks throughout the city while Ford Model A cars drive by in the opposite direction.

The streetcar travels north on Oneida Street, east on College Avenue with downtown in plain sight, past the tree-lined Lawrence University campus area, north on Rankin Street, east on Pacific Street to Riverside Cemetery and back downtown.

Along the way, passersby are seen both escaping the path of the car as well as waiting for its arrival and hitching on for a ride. Familiar buildings are shown, as well as others now gone. The passengers seen getting on the car were some of the very last passengers to ever ride a streetcar in Appleton. After the 11:40 p.m. run later that evening, the time of the electric streetcar in Appleton was over.

The electric streetcar gliding up and down Appleton's streets was the vision of Judge J.E. Harriman, who took a trip to Montgomery, Alabama, in the spring of 1886, specifically to observe an experiment to be attempted there by a Belgian engineer, Charles Van Depoele, with a streetcar, a power station and a half-mile track. The experiment was a mild success, as doubts remained whether enough electricity could be generated and transmitted to sustain a track of any practical distance.

Harriman, however, had no doubts at all. He was an Appletonian, after all, from a place where waterpower was creating an industrial empire that was now lighting a city. He went back to Appleton and within weeks rounded up six other investors for a total of $35,000 to give to Van Depoele to build a track over four miles long.

Anticipation was rampant in the city for the opening of the track. The residents watched the lines being laid and knew Appleton would become the first city in the nation to open public transportation via electric streetcar. Other states, such as Alabama and Virginia, had cities that had constructed experimental tracks, but none had yet maintained a commercial enterprise utilizing such. Five streetcars were on order to be built by the Pullman Car Company in Chicago, and delays in production were said to be of "considerable annoyance."

When the date was set for the initial run on August 16, 1886, the world was watching. Prominent street railway men and electricians from Boston, New York, Detroit, Cleveland and many other cities throughout the nation arrived in Appleton to witness the event. Nowhere else had a car run four miles without horses.

Interurban line on Commercial Street in Neenah, circa 1910. Russell House and Neenah City Hall, both William Waters designs, seen in background. *Courtesy of the Neenah Public Library.*

Charles Van Depoele was in attendance as well and pulled the lever that transmitted the electric current, powered by a hydroelectric power plant that was located off John Street adjacent to the river, through two overhead trolley wires running with the track, down to a connecting wire on the streetcar and ultimately to the motor attached to the car's front end. The run was a success, and the Appleton Electric Street Railway Company, presided over by J.E. Harriman, forever entered the record books.

Their time, however, was not long-lived. The early days of electric streetcars had many disadvantages. The streets, most of them at least, were not paved. Dirt, rocks and various other debris would often cause cars to jump the tracks, creating delays. Steep hills were always an adventure for the cars, which were housed in a facility on the site of the current Gabriel Furniture Building on College Avenue, as were snow and rain, which would often cause the service to have to be temporarily shut down.

Just four years after a world-famous success, in 1890, the Appleton Electric Railway Company went bankrupt.

A year later, the Appleton Edison Electric Company, which was basically the new and improved Appleton Edison Light Company, revised the streetcar service and many of the initial challenges were overcome. More roads were paved, the cars were bigger, the tracks were better and residents began to see

Streetcar waiting for passengers outside Krueger's Hardware on Wisconsin Avenue in Neenah, circa 1915. The Bergstrom Paper smokestack rises behind. *Courtesy of the Neenah Public Library.*

Automobiles outside of Krueger's Hardware on Wisconsin Avenue in Neenah, circa 1930s, after the streetcars were obsolete. *Courtesy of the Neenah Public Library.*

the streetcars as a viable form of transportation again, which led the rest of the Fox Cities to explore adding the service. The carbarn was also moved from College Avenue into the industrial flats, on present Olde Oneida Street.

Beginning in Oshkosh in 1894, a plan was commenced for running an interurban line from Oshkosh, north to Neenah-Menasha, continuing to Appleton, and finally Green Bay. The plan was thwarted by corporate red tape, leaving the Neenah and Menasha Electric Railway Company to expand the lines south, which then morphed into the Fox River Valley Electric Railway Company. Interurban lines were finally expanded into Neenah-Menasha in 1898 and Kaukauna in 1902.

Ridership on the electric streetcars skyrocketed as the cities on the lower Fox River continued to form one community. Traveling within the Fox Cities was, for the first time, no longer a virtual daylong affair. People were now able to live farther away from business districts, leading to neighborhoods and smaller communities forming on the outskirts of town. Businesses were helped exponentially, as their consumer market grew out to the rural areas as well. By 1918, residents in the Fox Cities made their local electric transit system the heaviest utilized in the state, over Milwaukee, which had initiated an electric streetcar rail system in 1890.

Streetcar in snow, Kaukauna, circa 1922. *Courtesy of the Kaukauna Public Library.*

The world again took its lead from Appleton. Charles Van Depoele was in high demand, sought out by rail companies in Boson and Detroit, among others. By 1900, just fourteen years after J.E. Harriman's inaugural run on a short, four-and-a-half-mile track along unpaved, rough-cut roads, cities in America were maintaining over sixteen thousand miles of electric railway.

By 1927, the Wisconsin-Michigan Power Company owned the rail system in the Fox Cities and was focusing its attention away from electric transit, as the company saw the future coming on the horizon. The reputation of the rail companies took a hit due to labor unrest and rumors, true as they were, of rampant corruption; widespread government regulations began to make running and maintaining the rails unprofitable; and gas-powered consumer automobiles and mass transit busses soon made the electric streetcar obsolete. The interurban lines were the first to be abandoned. Then the local tracks. The electric streetcars provided their last day of service in Appleton on April 6, 1930, when a camera was mounted on the front of the car to document the literal end of an era.

Today, little else remains in the valley of the days of the streetcar. The tracks have been dug up or paved over through the decades. The cars themselves were sold, dismantled or sent back to the manufacturer long ago. Rumors have persisted for years that some are sitting around in the Fox Cities in yards, used as playsets for children or makeshift trailers, but simply rumors they remain.

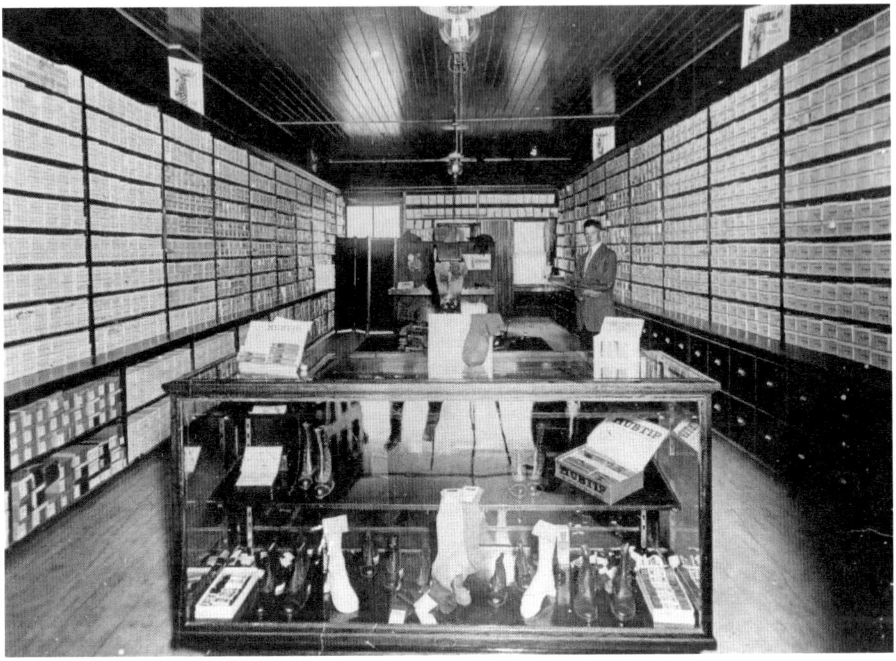

Interior of Tuchscherer's Shoe Store on Main Street, a Menasha institution for one hundred years standing opposite the Menasha Hotel, 1912. H.J. Tuchscherer Jr. stands in the 1887 building that would burn in 1940. The structure would be rebuilt, and the store continue to operate until 1987. *Courtesy of the Menasha Public Library.*

Along Olde Oneida Street in Appleton, on the front of an otherwise nondescript, cream brick building with a middle garage door, a historical marker mounted under cracks in the facade, reads,

> *On August 16, 1886 the Appleton Electric Street Railway Company began operation of the world's first commercially successful electric street railway. The cars were driven by Van Depoele direct current motors which received power from a hydroelectric generator through two trolley wires. In 1930, the expanded electric street railway system serving the cities of Appleton, Neenah, Menasha and Kaukauna was retired when bus service was begun to better serve the transportation needs of these communities.*

It was on this site, now converted office space called the Edison Building, that the streetcars were housed and started and ended their day. The building lies adjacent to a redeveloped area named Trolley Square, inside of which sits a refurbished Birney Streetcar.

Wheeler Transfer Line in Menasha, circa 1920. Freight haulers and one of the area's first Ford automobile dealers. *Courtesy of the Menasha Public Library.*

Due to a further surge of immigration, along with new technologies of faster, more convenient modes of transportation, a new wave of political and social groups began to form, linking neighborhoods throughout the valley while also establishing new identities as American capitalists. Small businesses were started, goods were bought and sold and commerce began its transformation of the individual Fox Cities into one collective community.

The setting for such gatherings of the day, in which political, commercial, religious and social issues were negotiated and events took place, was usually a hotel, or more specifically, a luxury hotel. A hotel showcasing the latest in technology and conveniences represented a certain status for the city. To be a city of significance and importance, a municipality needed a fancy hotel.

One community that began to flourish during the latter part of the nineteenth century was Menasha. Business and industry rapidly increased in the city with aggressive local leadership and an influx of innovative and resourceful entrepreneurship, led by George Whiting and William Gilbert, among others. Along with paper and wood-product manufacturers,

Menasha's downtown business district would experience its own growth spurt, culminating in a modern urban commercial thoroughfare to complement its evolving and ever-growing population.

One of the earlier post–Civil War structures on Menasha's Main Street was the National Hotel, built in 1869 by Reuben Scott, a real estate speculator who went on to also raise the first paper mill in Menasha in 1876, along with numerous other structures of early Menasha. Built on the southwest corner of Main and Mill Streets, the National Hotel was really the first structure to signal Menasha's expanding prominence, as the hotel was built with the finest amenities of luxury for the day. Featuring hot and cold baths, a billiards room, bar and "fronts on the lake," the hotel had accommodations for ten guests, being a smaller, more intimate place of stay, and charged two dollars per day with discounts for nurses and children.

The hotel was the setting for a meeting of investors on February 4, 1871, that included Curtis Reed, the founder of Menasha, and his brother, George, who was a Manitowoc County judge and strong supporter of railroads and was exploring options for a line running from Menasha into the Northwoods. It was in the hotel on that date that the Wisconsin Central Railroad was formally organized and contracts were awarded.

Reuben Scott was contracted to build the first leg of the track from Menasha west to Steven's Point, where it would then turn north to Ashland, and according to the *History of Wisconsin: The Civil War Era, 1848–1873*, in doing so, "set something of a construction record," as he laid sixty-three miles of track in only 120 days. The first train set off on October 2, 1871, and the tracks reached Ashland in 1877, expanding farther into Chippewa Falls and Minneapolis after further years of delays and red tape.

The organization of the Wisconsin Central was important in regard to timber and passenger traffic, which led not only to further prominence for Menasha, as transportation south to the Fox Cities was now much more practical, but also for the Northwoods, as communities there began to rise around the railroad. The Wisconsin Central Railroad was dissolved when it was purchased by the Soo Line in the 1960s and in October 2001 became part of Canadian National, which it remains today.

By 1901, the National Hotel was past its prime. Tourists and travel had centralized in Appleton and Oshkosh, and the hotel was feeling the pinch. In the early morning hours of October 23, George Reed, who was now the proprietor of the National Hotel, noticed flames in the building, and they

Main Street view of the Menasha Hotel in the 1970s, well after its glory days. Tuchscherer's Shoe Store, named Tuk-Cher's by then, stands opposite; it was razed in the 1990s. *Courtesy of the Menasha Public Library.*

were rapidly rising. Wasting no time, Reed immediately raced to find the porter, and the two of them fought through the smoke, heat and flames to reach every room, enabling all thirty guests to safely escape. By the time the local fire departments of Menasha and Neenah arrived, the building, and everything in it, was lost.

The widow of Reuben Scott, who died in 1890, said she would not rebuild. For the first time in thirty years, Menasha was without a first-class hotel. Today, the Scott Block at 180 Main Street remains the only structure remaining built by one of Menasha's most prominent early commercial pioneers.

The city of Menasha, however, did not believe it could survive without a luxury hotel. The business community felt it was vital to maintain its status as a manufacturing center and, without much delay, a plan was put into action. The Menasha Hotel Association pulled no punches, hiring William Waters to design the three-story, redbrick structure trimmed with Bedford stone.

Main Street, downtown Menasha, 1880s. The National Hotel is seen on the right. *Courtesy of the Neenah Public Library.*

Same view of Main Street, downtown Menasha, 1940s. The Menasha Hotel is seen on the right. *Courtesy of the Neenah Public Library.*

At 2:00 p.m. on September 11, 1905, all factories and businesses were closed so all the city could be present to see the laying of the cornerstone of the new Hotel Menasha along with a time capsule containing currency denominations, photographs and several newspapers of the day. Several thousand people attended the event, complete with a military band.

On Saturday, May 5, 1906, a grand opening, ten-course banquet was held at the new pride of the city. Hosted by William Gilbert, the gala proved an "immense success." About 150 guests attended, mostly industry and business insiders from Chicago, Milwaukee, Racine, Sheboygan and throughout the Fox Cities, who all got a tour of the latest in upscale hospitality.

The interior of the Menasha Hotel was "more elegant in its furnishings than any other in this vicinity." The lobby was graced with a front counter of Italian marble, tile floors, and was finished, along with the adjacent dining room, in quartered oak. The forty guest chambers on the second and third floors all contained polished hardwood floors, and the rooms were finished in elegant birch. Electricity and gas were wired in, and each room had a telephone, unusual for the period. The hotel's success was immediate, leading to William Waters making additions in 1911 and again in 1916, doubling the capacity of the hotel.

As was the case in the days of the National Hotel, however, Menasha couldn't hide from its limits. The Hotel Menasha started seeing business fall off as Appleton, Neenah and Oshkosh cornered the traveler's market. The establishment changed hands numerous times in the late twentieth century, finally being converted to apartments for elderly residents in the 1980s.

In 2014, a very public battle was fought between private developers who had purchased the building and the Menasha Landmarks Commission involving the property. The team of new owners, led by local entrepreneur John Bergstrom, the great-great-grandson of D.W. Bergstrom, was looking to redevelop the location, which would entail the razing of the 110-year-old hotel, then known as River's Edge Apartments and Historic Hotel Pub. In the end, the state of Main Street's current economic vitality won out over nostalgia, and the old hotel, along with the neighboring 1917 First National Bank building, were taken down. Two years later, the eight-story, 118,000-square-foot One Menasha Center office tower rose up over the city, the first time in almost 150 years a hotel did not occupy that spot.

In its September 7, 1915 edition, the *Oshkosh Northwestern* had a small, somewhat obscure, page 11 article announcing the accepted plans of a new hotel in Neenah. The subheading reads, "Structure Planned for City of

George Edwin Bergstrom's lone local design, the Valley Inn. Built in 1916, it was the center of city activity for fifty years before being razed in the 1960s. A modern hotel now stands on the site. *Courtesy of the Neenah Public Library.*

Neenah Will Meet All Demands for an Up-to-Date Building." The architect of this new hotel was of international prominence, but of local roots. George Edwin Bergstrom, already renowned at the time, was coming home to design what was to be the city's finest hotel, the Valley Inn. Bergstrom was the eldest son of George O. Bergstrom, owner of Bergstrom Stove Works, and the nephew of D.W. Bergstrom, founder of the Bergstrom Paper Company.

Born in Neenah in 1879, Edwin Bergstrom graduated from Neenah High School and went on to attend Phillips-Andover Academy in Andover, Massachusetts. After attending Yale for one year, he transferred to the Massachusetts Institute of Technology, graduating in 1899, and soon moved west, settling in Los Angeles, where he married the daughter of J.A. Kimberly, cofounder of Neenah's Kimberly-Clark & Company.

While in Los Angeles, Bergstrom was responsible for much of the city's early downtown, designing buildings such as the Brownstone Hotel, Bullock's Department Store, Citizens Bank Building, Ford Motor Company Building, LA Athletic Club and many more, all before designing his hometown's hotel.

On the night of Saturday, September 9, 1916, a "get-together gathering" took place celebrating the opening of the Valley Inn, which was referred to as the "finest building of its kind in the state today." An open house for the general public was held for inspection of the premises the next day, and the hotel officially opened that following Monday morning, September 11, 1916. The first floor featured a massive main dining hall, two private dining rooms, a bar, large French windows, suspended outdoor light globes and a wraparound uncovered porch along three sides of the building. The second and third floors held sixty rooms, thirty private bathrooms and additional women's sewing and powder rooms. For the next fifty years, the hotel was the center for civic and social gatherings in Neenah, providing first-class accommodations when Neenah was looking to roll out a red carpet.

Edwin Bergstrom went on to continue his illustrious career in Los Angeles, designing the Pasadena Civic Auditorium and Convention Center, Grauman's Metropolitan Theatre (later the Paramount Theatre) and the Los Angeles County Hospital, a massive complex known in popular culture as the setting for the soap opera *General Hospital.*

In 1941, Bergstrom turned his attention back east as he was tabbed by the U.S. Department of Defense to consolidate the many defense agencies

Hotel Appleton, corner of Appleton and Washington Streets, circa 1950. Built in 1893 as the Ritger Hotel, it was demolished in 1961 for new construction. *Courtesy of the Andrew J. Mueller Collection at the History Museum at the Castle.*

spread throughout the Greater D.C. area into one building. Along with his associate David Witmer, Edwin Bergstrom completed the general design of the Pentagon in only five days in July 1941. Construction began on the building on September 11 of that year, thirty years to the day from the grand opening of his sole hometown work and, in an eerie coincidence, sixty years to the day before the building was attacked by a hijacked airplane in 2001.

After several decades, time began to take its toll on the Valley Inn. In 1967, Sam Pickard, president of the National Manufacturers Bank and then owner of the hotel, announced he was looking to redevelop the site as the hotel was "no longer sufficiently modern enough to attract visitors" and was losing money. No fight was put up by the city, and the once grand hotel was demolished later that year. The location has remained the premier hotel site in the city, however, and now showcases the modern Riverwalk Hotel, built on the same ground as George Edwin Bergstrom's only local structure.

In November 1929, Appleton, which had its fair share of hotels, turned its attention to arts and recreation with the opening of a modern theater to showcase a new technology that was sweeping the nation at the time: talkies. The Fox Theater, which was built on the site of an old vaudeville theater named the Bijou, installed the latest equipment to provide the best possible sound quality of the day. The November 15 edition of the *Post-Crescent* boasts that "Appleton has the latest, the best, and the most perfect theater yet for the presentation of sound pictures."

The walls of the theater were treated with a "special acoustic plaster which aids in the reproduction of sound" in an attempt at an early form of surround sound. The fabrics in the theater, the chairs, the curtains and drapes were even selected based on their acoustical integrity. Sound engineering for "talkies" was still in its beginning stages, though the Fox Theater in Appleton was equipped with the highest-end technologies yet installed anywhere.

On opening night, Appleton rolled out the red carpet for its new theater, as the "Master showman of New York" arrived for the event. Joe Leo, the president of Fox Metropolitan, a chain of East Coast theaters, was in Appleton to christen the Fox, which "stands as the most modern in the country."

They Had to See Paris, featuring Will Rogers, was projected onto the screen, and the sound was supplied by a fifteen-inch record synched up with the film. Not one of the over 1,700 seats in the theater was empty.

The interior of the theater was designed to resemble the Alhambra in Granada, Spain, a Moorish palace built by the Muslim rulers of Spain and

Rio Theater, circa 1955. *Courtesy of the Andrew J. Mueller Collection at the History Museum at the Castle.*

later the royal court of Ferdinand and Isabella—a tall order for a building in Appleton, Wisconsin, though the Fox pulled out all the stops.

The floors in the foyer of the theater were intricately designed mosaic tile, gleaming with red, blue and gold hues. Large hand-carved wooden furniture in fourteenth-century style lined the walls below wrought-iron lighting sconces, amid drapery, tapestries and silk shawls imported directly from the Middle East. The ceiling of the auditorium was painted a rich, midnight blue, complete with stars above the walls painted to resemble a Moorish garden, with tall vines, flowers and trees leading one's eye to more silken shawls draped over the balconies. "Appleton has something to be proud of," the papers exclaimed. "It is the last word in theaters."

The theater that the Fox replaced, however, was not so well received twenty-five years earlier. When H.C. Danforth of the Bijou Amusement Company announced it had leased property at 119 North Oneida Street, just one block off College Avenue in downtown Appleton, for the erection of a vaudeville theater, residents were not having it. Letters were sent in to the city council, and small protests were held over concern that the shows, especially those held on Sundays, would not be kept "clean." Danforth himself appeared before the city council and claimed that "all performances at its theaters are clean and wholesome and that nothing is ever said or done at any of the performances which can be criticized by the most fastidious." Danforth then invited the council to set up a panel to judge the Bijou's performances and pledged a certified check for $500 "to be donated to public charity if at anytime anything is said or done at any of the Bijou Theaters which may be considered degrading or detrimental to the public morals."

By 1920, the Bijou failed to remain profitable and sat empty for several years until reopened by a Green Bay entrepreneur, who kept the name. It was during this brief second run that movies with sound, however choppy and unsynchronized that it was, began to be popular, though the building was soon sold to Fox Metropolitan, which razed the Bijou and built the Fox in 1929.

By 1933, the building had been sold to the Appleton Building Company, which affiliated the theater with Warner Bros. and rebranded the movie palace as the Rio, its moniker for twenty-six years.

By 1959, the recreational habits of Americans had changed. Retail shopping and department stores had pried attention away from the glamorous movie houses of the classic Hollywood era, and the Rio was sold to the H.C. Prange Company, which was building an adjacent six-story department store, for use as an annex for appliances, televisions and radios. Three years later, Prange's announced it would raze the building to utilize the space for a parking ramp. The once most "perfect and modern" movie palace in the country was soon a pile of concrete, steel and bricks. The building was barely thirty-five years old. Accounts of passersby at the time speak of glancing through the rubble and seeing old silken shawls waving in the open air.

Just one block north of the Rio was the Appleton Theatre, built in 1901 as the city's "new" opera house and constructed specifically for stage

Four women in front of poster for *Little Women*, showing at the Appleton Theatre, 1914. *Courtesy of the Kaukauna Public Library.*

productions. The building of the Appleton was a joint effort by several local entrepreneurs of the day, including John Van Nortwick, owner of the Appleton Pulp and Paper Company, and hotelier John Conway. Accounts of the theater's grand opening in February 1902 are documented in papers of the day as a rousing success and began with a production of *Nathan Hale*, the title character being played by Wisconsin-born Howard Kyle.

What was not always a rousing success, however, were some of the later productions in the playhouse, and the reviewers of the day were quite colorful about them, as in this review from April 1902, in the *Post-Crescent*:

> *Was Not So Warm*
>
> *"The Hottest Coon in Dixie," at the Appleton Theatre last evening, was not so warm. In fact, it was not nearly so hot as were some of the people it separated from their 25, 35, or 50 cents as the case might be. The performance was pretty good in spots, but the spots were not thick. There were one or two good negro voices, and several of the other kind.*

Main Street in Kimberly, view looking north circa 1910. *Courtesy of the Kimberly Public Library.*

Corner of Wisconsin Avenue and Desnoyer Street, Kaukauna, circa 1880. *Courtesy of the Kaukauna Public Library.*

The dancing can be discounted any day on any Mississippi steamboat deck. There is much more that could be said about the performance, but "knocking" is cheap amusement—and our hammer is mislaid, anyway.

After several decades of unmatched success in the city as a venue for stage productions, the Appleton was later rebranded as a movie theater as film began to supplant the stage as the preferred platform of entertainment. Attendance began to slow when entertainment venues began to be moved away from the downtown area in the 1950s and '60s and new, more modern movie theaters were built on Oneida Street and Northland Avenue, now the Grand Meridian banquet hall. The building was eventually sold to the First Federal Savings and Loan Association.

Outliving its former neighbor, the Rio, by thirteen years, the Appleton Theatre was razed in 1972, again for a parking lot. At one point in the mid-twentieth century, Appleton boasted no less then five theaters, all downtown. Their names still elicit memories from the older generation: the Rio, Elite, Majestic, Appleton and Viking. All are now gone.

Konrad Brothers Dry Goods & Groceries Store, Kaukauna, 1895. *Courtesy of the Kaukauna Public Library.*

Menasha Fire Station–City Hall Building, built in 1885 at 124 Main Street. Abandoned by the city in 1979 and razed for new construction in 1989. *Courtesy of the Menasha Public Library.*

At the turn of the century, commercial development in the Fox Cites began to propel the community forward as a desired destination for entrepreneurs and small business owners. The spirit of enterprise had never been so pronounced, and the persistent efforts of prominent business owners to work to continue the rapid increase of community integration fueled further industrial expansion.

Chambers of commerce were started. Business organizations spearheading community outreach and promotion of the Fox Cities as a successful commercial district were activated. Small business leaders, from boardinghouse proprietors to dry goods and general merchandise store managers, stepped up their involvement in local politics, as they lobbied for improved roads leading from rural areas and increased access to electric street cars and the interurban lines.

Downtown architecture transformed from crude, wood-framed structures to grand stone and brick buildings with ornate, intricate detailing designed by the finest Wisconsin architects of the day, such as William Waters and Charles Hove. Business districts in Kaukauna, Kimberly, Menasha,

Little Chute and Neenah became clearly defined, supporting their local economies, both in concert with and independent from the larger cities of Appleton and Oshkosh.

One pillar of downtown architecture in the Fox Cities was built by Charles Hove in Appleton in 1882 for a German-language newspaper called the *Appleton Volksfreund*. The building became known locally, even in more recent times long after the paper ended publication, as the Volksfreund Building. The structure was of Italianate style with an imposing, ornate corner tower. A photograph, silhouette or drawing of the structure often graced the covers of marketing and promotional literature, annual reports and other print material regarding the commercial district of downtown Appleton, its familiar cupola becoming a symbol of Appleton itself.

The building was erected by H.W. Meyers, the publisher of the newspaper that had outgrown its current building. A large contingent of German-born immigrants had settled in the Fox Cities around that time, brought here by opportunities of employment in saw or paper mills, canal and dam building, farming or various other ventures. Although immigrants were proudly becoming American, difficulties fully understanding the language persisted,

Volksfreund Building, circa 1892. This downtown Appleton landmark burned to the ground in 1981. *Courtesy of the Appleton Public Library.*

which oftentimes led to preventable misunderstandings regarding the political and social issues of the day. Because of this, the *Appleton Volksfreund* was founded in 1870, published as a weekly edition assisting its readers in adapting to a new American landscape.

Unlike other local papers, the *Volksfreund* placed correspondents in every municipality in the Fox Cities—villages, towns, and cities—and encouraged subscribers to talk with these correspondents about various issues and hot-button topics that were then published in the paper, a sort of early form of internet comment threads. The paper was widely read in every surrounding county, having eight thousand subscribers, which was a gigantic number for the day.

By 1882, Meyer began construction of his new building on the northeast corner of College Avenue and Morrison Street. He placed his printing presses in the basement of the building and utilized the second story for the editorial offices. The first floor was reserved for retail.

Arnold Peerenboom, a young entrepreneur just entering business for himself, rented the first floor of the new building to run a clothing and dry goods store, the first of close to one hundred years of commercial retailers to utilize the prime downtown location. H.W. Meyer himself ran a music store out of the building as well, selling violins, accordions, guitars and the "largest selection of sheet music in the Fox Cities."

Both the paper and Peerenboom's thrived at the location for decades. H.W. Meyer's son eventually inherited the *Appleton Volksfreund* from his late father and moved its offices one block north in 1919, to the southwest corner of Washington and Morrison Streets. The paper slowly began to fade as second-generation German Americans had no need for the native-language publication and rural postal routes dramatically improved, increasing circulation of the daily newspapers. It ceased publication in 1932.

Peerenboom remained for thirty-five years, retiring in 1917. Throughout the decades, the building was home to numerous retail ventures, including two Appleton commercial institutions, Galpin Hardware Store and W.A. Close clothiers.

On the morning of April 8, 1981, the first call to the fire department came in at 4:24 a.m. Minutes later, as the thirty-five firefighters arrived on scene, flames were billowing out the second floor of the Volksfreund Building as the roof was about to cave in. The city landmark's iconic corner cupola had to be taken down with a crane so it would not fall on those battling the blaze. By noon, only the four outside walls were standing. The ceilings, roof and inside walls, along with all the building's contents, were smoldering inside of them. The Volksfreund Building, which had watched over College Avenue from its corner on Morrison Street for ninety-nine years, was no more.

The city and its surrounding neighbors were shocked and saddened. Virtually nobody alive knew Appleton without it and therefore never saw College Avenue without the elegant 1882 Charles Hove masterpiece. As the heat from the fire cooled, and the black smoke that hovered over Appleton's main thoroughfare drifted away, a headline in the *Appleton Post-Crescent,* published later on the afternoon of the building's tragic and sudden destruction, read, "A Piece of Appleton Dies."

W.A. Close erected a new building on the site and reopened the clothing store in November 1981, a triumphant return for one of the city's most tragic losses. The rebuilt structure remains today as a law firm, as the clothing store ended operations in 1995.

WILLIAM WATERS

In 1867, twenty-four-year-old William Waters left the only home he'd ever known, in Franklin, New York, and traveled to Oshkosh, with not much more in tow than his dreams. After attaining only about three semesters of higher education at Rensselaer Polytechnic Institute in Troy, New York, Waters apparently figured that was enough and went on to Oshkosh, establishing a small architectural firm that same year.

It was not happenstance that Waters chose to come to Oshkosh, but rather a calculated professional strategy. For one, Oshkosh was a very wealthy city, as lumber was still king, and opportunity was there for the taking. More so, however, few cities in the nation at that time were in such need of architectural services as Oshkosh, which had just suffered through a string of devastating fires and, unbeknownst to Waters at the time, was about to be hit with more.

The entire city of Oshkosh at the midpoint of the nineteenth century was virtual kindling. Lumber was stacked for miles along the sawmills lining the Fox River. Wood-frame houses dotted the city, and wood made up just about every other erected structure, as stone and brick were seldom yet utilized.

In May 1859, the first of Oshkosh's "great fires" took out the entire business district, six blocks on both sides of Ferry Street, current Main Street. With a blaze starting in an unused barn on the corner of Ceape and State Streets, wind blew the flames directly through the neighboring blocks, covering them with smoldering stacks of burnt-out wooden buildings; 125 in all were lost. Incredibly, nobody was killed in the blaze, as it occurred

Oshkosh State Normal School, circa 1887. Built in 1869, the building was destroyed by fire in 1916. Dempsey Hall now occupies the site. *Courtesy of the Oshkosh Public Library.*

in the early morning hours and the mostly commercial buildings were unoccupied at the time.

Just one month later, seventy new buildings had been rebuilt and business and commerce resumed in the downtown district. The majority of these new buildings, however, were wooden.

In May 1866, history repeated itself. Another fire, this time starting in a dental office on Ferry Street, spread throughout the business district. Leaving a heap of charred wood in their wake, the flames were subdued only after a heavy downpour arrived mercifully from the skies just as the fire began raging toward a residential area.

Again, not a life was lost as the fire began around 1:00 a.m. and most homes were spared, almost as if a second warning were cast toward the city of raw lumber and sawdust. The *Oshkosh Northwestern* noted at the time, "It was entirely a wooden range with no walls of brick or stone to check the flames and give the firemen a chance."

Soon after, the Oshkosh Common Council announced that wooden buildings would no longer be allowed to be constructed within the business districts of the city. William Waters arrived in Oshkosh months later, undoubtedly lured by such a tantalizing ordinance.

By 1868, Waters had settled in, opened his firm and married Catherine Follett, the daughter of a former mayor of the city, which likely assisted in his gaining ground inside political circles, leading to several civic commissions. Oshkosh was awarded the site of the state normal school in that year, edging out numerous other suitors for the teacher training facility, including Neenah. The *Northwestern* announced in March 1869 that the state had procured a seven-acre location overlooking the river and the city for the building and "is under the efficient superintendence of Mr. Wm. Waters of this city, Architect and builder."

The normal school building stood 75 by 126 feet, facing Algoma Boulevard, and opened for the 1871 school year. Built of cream-colored Calumet brick and blue limestone, it stood four stories high, with an imposing center tower reaching 144 feet into the sky. The walls of the school were sixteen inches thick, of solid brick, with 700,000 of them used in the building's construction. Numerous additions to the normal school were made over the decades, most handled by Waters. The initial 1871 building was soon just a small section of a much larger complex that ultimately became the University of Wisconsin–Oshkosh.

In the late-night hours of March 22, 1916, the normal school caught fire. This time, the thick brick and limestone were acting as a firewall for a while, though another problem ensued: a water main that fed the standpipes in the school was broken, leaving water shooting out and negating the water pressure to the fire hoses fighting the blaze. Witnesses said the water streams weren't even able to reach the second-story windows. The building burned for over twenty-four hours, as the fire department made repeated trips to the school for fires that were breaking out in the ruins. The *Oshkosh Northwestern* of March 23, 1916, notes:

> *The scene of the ruins today is pathetic. Where stood the old stately building blackened and tottering walls, and in the smoking ruins somewhere is a safe supposed to be fireproof and filled with valuable records and papers. The campus and street are filled with slush and considerable work has been necessary to make the street passable.*

Sam Hay residence on Jackson Street and Algoma Boulevard, Oshkosh. Built by Waters in 1873, it was salvaged and razed in the 1940s. *Courtesy of the Winnebago County Historical and Archaeological Society.*

The 151,000-square-foot Dempsey Hall was built on the former site of the normal school in 1918 and still stands there today.

By 1874, Waters's architectural business was in great demand, not only in Oshkosh but throughout the Fox Cities. Appleton, Neenah and Menasha had all had commercial buildings, schools, banks and private residences added to their cityscapes by the hand of William Waters, who was by this point the most sought-after architect in the region.

Oshkosh's downtown business districts were being rebuilt with brick, mortar and stone, much by the work of Waters, but old wooden buildings still remained, as they were "grandfathered" out of the city ordinances—quite of few of them, actually.

Two fires in 1874, one in May and one in July, again devastated the city, wiping out further businesses and homes, both of the wealthy and of the working man. The July fire caused the death of a well-known and respected citizen, Billy Taylor, who died assisting a handicapped woman to safety, the first documented fatality of the city's "great fires."

One of the private residences built by Waters during this time period was for Samuel M. Hay, a prominent business and civic leader and former mayor of Oshkosh. S.M. Hay was an owner of the Hay Hardware company, for which Waters also designed commercial buildings, and was also a banker for forty years, being the organizer and president of the First National Bank of Oshkosh.

The Hay residence was built at the corner of Algoma Boulevard and Jackson Street in 1873. The large, brick, two-story home was centered with a three-and-a-half-story tower and observation window, from which Hay would watch his downtown businesses burn to the ground just two years later in the worst fire in Oshkosh's history. His wife, Maria, would pass away in the home forty-eight hours after that.

After S.M. Hay's death in 1906, his daughter, Mary Hay Caldwell, an Oshkosh socialite, and her family lived in the home until 1924, after which further deaths in the family left the home abandoned. The home was sold in the 1940s to a salvage company in Fond du Lac to be taken down piece by piece, as the house remained in excellent physical condition. During the salvage period, mint-condition marble fireplaces and solid oak doors and paneling were removed, still displaying the intricate details and craftsmanship known to be in a Waters-designed home. There was no planned building project at the time the house was taken down, and today the site is used as a parking lot.

In 1875, Waters's work volume increased rapidly in Oshkosh, but not so much in the rest of the Fox Valley. The reason for this is clear, yet sobering, as after April 28, 1875, Oshkosh barely had a city left at all.

As stated previously, the Great Fire of 1875 started in the Morgan Brothers' lumberyard on that fateful day in April, but the Morgan Brothers mill was not operating that day, nor were any others due to the wind and dry conditions. Any others, that is, except for one. Spalding and Peck, which was a lumber mill adjacent to Morgan Brothers, was operating that day, and sparks from one of its furnaces were blown over into Morgan's yard and ignited a pile of lumber.

As James Metz recounts in his masterfully researched *Oshkosh Aflame!: Traumas and Triumphs of Its Sawdust Citizens*, the words of the city editor of the *Northwestern*, Charles Bowron, convey a gripping sense of desperation:

> *On came the rushing tide of flame, more furious than the descending floods of Mill river. The steamers were powerless to check such a furious adversary. No sooner could they get set and at work than the enemy would charge with*

Tremont House, circa 1887. Rebuilt by Waters after the fire of 1875, the building fell into disrepair and was razed in 1962. *Courtesy of the Oshkosh Public Library.*

> *bayonets of fire and drive them from their work. It soon became apparent that it must sweep everything before it, and the merchants of Main Street began to more seriously consider the situation. In less than 20 minutes, the fire had swept from Morgan's mill to the Milwaukee and St Paul depot and freight house, and they were swept away like leaves on a blast furnace.*

The recent progress in fire protection and building codes were no match for the infernos that were fed constantly by stacked lumberyards and grandfathered wooden buildings. Four hours after the fire that killed Thomas Davis as he attempted to save vital company records began in the Morgan mill, the wind subdued, and it was over. The commercial district of the city was literally burned out. Scores of residences were gone. Two people were dead. Oshkosh was again in ruins.

The day after the fire, on April 29, carpenters were seen framing a two-story-high structure. One of the greatest rebuilds in the nation's history was already underway.

William Waters received a multitude of commissions after the fire, twenty of which were listed in one article regarding the rebuild of Main Street in the *Northwestern* on July 15, 1875, which states only two lots had yet to begin erecting a building. "The energy and promptness displayed immediately after the fire was astonishing and has given to Oshkosh a reputation for enterprise and zeal which will stick to her to the end of time."

Banks, hardware stores, grocers, furniture stores, cigar dealers, confectionaries and shoe salesmen were hiring Waters to design and build their new stores on Main Street. The district was transformed from wooden structures with occasional brick neighbors to entire rows of elegant brick buildings with show windows, double doors, intricate detail, high pediments, columns, pillars and iron cornices reminiscent of any high-society downtown in America.

At this time, Waters also rebuilt the Tremont House on the corner of Waugoo and State Streets, which survived the fire though badly damaged. It was originally built soon after the Civil War, and Waters improved the Tremont to a 5,600-square-foot, three-story hotel containing forty rooms and all the modern conveniences of the day. The Tremont catered to traveling commercial salesmen, who would stay at the hotel with eight to ten trunks full of merchandise which they would sell, directly out of the trunks, in large sample rooms in the hotel.

The Tremont House opened just five months after the fire, and Oshkosh once again was able to boast a first-class hotel. The main floor contained a

Roberts' Resort, circa 1883. Once the preeminent local vacation getaway on Doty Island, it was razed in 1965 for new construction. *Courtesy of the Neenah Public Library.*

large dining room, parlors, sitting rooms and a modern washroom featuring marble bowls and silver-plated faucets supplying soft water from a reservoir, the latest in amenities for the day. The second and third floors held the private rooms, "as handsomely and elegantly fitted and furnished as any hotel in this part of the state," according to the *Northwestern*. The rooms were furnished in black walnut, and each had its own unique pattern on beautiful, rich carpeting with sofas, easy chairs and cotton mattresses.

Over time, the hotel changed hands and names, ending as the State Hotel and falling into disrepair in the 1950s. It was demolished in 1962 to make way for a parking ramp for the Oshkosh National Bank. As with the Tremont, most of the commercial buildings along Main Street built by Waters also did not survive the twentieth century, as the phrase "Demolished for new construction" became commonplace, mainly after World War II.

Within mere months of the Great Fire of 1875, Oshkosh had made a miraculous recovery. In 1876, a correspondent from the *Chicago Commercial Advertiser* visited the city and wrote about what he saw in a September issue: "It was a year of such wonderful reconstruction as no city, except Chicago, ever witnessed. The main business street is entirely rebuilt and is now one of the finest commercial thoroughfares in the northwest. The Oshkosh people are peculiar. None but such as they could have built this beautiful town."

First National Bank on southwest corner of Wisconsin Avenue and Commercial Street in Neenah, circa 1920s. Razed in the 1930s for a more modern building. *Courtesy of the Neenah Historical Society.*

The Russell House Hotel, circa 1895. After it was destroyed in a fire in 1883, Waters rebuilt the hotel to a grand scale. The city hall can be seen behind it. *Courtesy of the Neenah Historical Society.*

By 1877, William Waters, whose blueprints had spearheaded that rebuild, once again began to take commissions outside of Oshkosh and turned his attention back to the Fox Cities, drawing plans for buildings in Appleton and Neenah. The first building Waters designed outside of Oshkosh after the fire was Roberts' Resort on Doty Island.

Commissioned by John Roberts, the manager of the National Hotel in Menasha, the resort was designed as a lakeside vacation spot, catering to a growing demand for leisurely activities outside of the burgeoning cities. Roberts had previously purchased the grounds formerly owned by Governor Doty on the island between Neenah and Menasha, and had the main building of the resort, designed by Waters, built right next to the original Doty cabin, about 150 yards to the east of where the re-created cabin stands today.

The main building was an elegant two-story structure with a piazza around the second floor "for the hungry returning fishermen…to sit, smoke, or chat looking out upon the broad lake expanse and tree, shrub, and floral adornment and in that quiet spot enjoy nature and rest to one's heart content." Interspersed throughout the forested grounds of oak, ash and elm were tennis courts, a golf course, private cabins and canoes along the shoreline. Doty's cabin was used in various aspects by the resort—from storage, to a billiard parlor and smoking room, to sleeping quarters for staff. Saturday nights, the resort was open to the public, as the dining room would be cleared and the locals from Neenah and Menasha, dressed to the nines, would regularly attend the entertainment for the evening.

After John Roberts's unexpected death in 1895, his family remained proprietors of the resort. An article in the *Northwestern* in 1904 portrays a still popular destination regularly attended by many of the local well-to-do, including the family of Nathan Paine, who was registered there at the time of the article. In 1905, however, the resort was sold to local entrepreneur John Strange and was converted into a private residence, the old Doty cabin being moved in 1948 to the location it currently occupies.

In 1965, later generations of the Strange family sold the grounds of the former resort for redevelopment. The main house built by Waters was offered to local historical societies, though due to costs of moving and maintenance of the property, they were forced to decline.

Roberts' Resort was razed in 1965. Modern houses now enjoy the view countless vacationers once did so many decades ago.

After the opening of Roberts' Resort, Neenah was hot on William Waters. Much of Neenah's downtown in the late nineteenth century was designed by Waters, as were many of the palatial homes of the city's elite.

Neenah City Hall, circa 1940s. All but the clock tower was razed in 1975. *Courtesy of the Neenah Public Library.*

Razing of Neenah City Hall, 1975. *Courtesy of the Neenah Historical Society.*

Kimberly-Clark office building. Built in 1880 and demolished in 1980. *Courtesy of the Neenah Public Library.*

In 1888, Waters built Neenah's city hall. Located on the corner of Commercial and Doty Streets, the building combined Ionic and Corinthian architectural styles, built of cream-colored pressed brick with a base of large cut stone blocks quarried from Duck Creek. A 12-foot-wide clock tower, rising 135 feet above the streets, watched over downtown. Two stone arches, one on Doty Avenue and one on Commercial Street, welcomed visitors and employees as they entered the building, leading to an 8-foot stairway with large oak banisters on either side with heavy Corinthian columns.

The imposing building held the jail, police and fire departments, city clerk, treasurer and all other municipal offices needed in a burgeoning city. "It can easily be said," exclaimed the *Oshkosh Times*, "that Winnebago County has no more attractive building than the Neenah city hall."

By the 1950s, however, Neenah's eye started to wander. The city began to outgrow its city hall, and the costs of maintaining the eighty-year-old landmark were outgrowing the costs to build a new one. The various municipal offices started utilizing temporary space in several other buildings until a new city hall was ultimately built in 1979.

While the old city hall remained empty, discussions ensued about what to do with it. It was fairly easily decided that most of the building would be razed, as it was simply too costly for the city or a potential buyer to maintain,

Washington School in Neenah. Built by Waters in 1879, it was razed in 1976. *Courtesy of the Neenah Historical Society.*

Neenah's Second Ward School, built by Waters in 1893. *Courtesy of the Neenah Historical Society.*

though saving the clock tower became a priority. Architects were brought in to survey the footings and the soil under the tower and deemed it structurally sound to remain standing, as it still does today. The rest of the building met the wrecker in 1975.

One of the structures that city hall used in the interim between moving out of the clock tower building and into a new one was also built by Waters. In 1972, the city moved government operations into the old Kimberly-Clark office building on Commercial Street.

In 1880, Kimberly-Clark had commissioned Waters to build its corporate office building, replacing the original wood-frame structure dating to 1872. Waters would go on to build mansions for two of Kimberly-Clark's founders, as well as numerous other paper barons in Neenah and Appleton. The structure served the company for decades, though when Kimberly-Clark vacated the almost one-hundred-year-old building, the city moved into the space, leaving it empty once again when the city's new complex was ready in 1979. Rumors had begun to swirl that the building would be razed, creating pause and concern from local historic preservation officials.

In the early morning hours of February 27, 1980, by cover of darkness, demolition crews arrived on the scene and began taking another one of William Waters's masterpieces apart. In a press release later that day, Kimberly-Clark stated that the rumors "gave every indication that the building would become an unresolvable controversy." The release went on, "We do not intend to be callous about architectural or historical interests, but if the hard choice has to be made between building for the future or preserving an expensive monument to the past, we believe that in this instance the future takes precedence."

By 1886, Waters had begun drawing up plans for what may be his best-known building.

With the boom of construction and rebuilding in the city over the previous decade and a half, the then second-largest city in Wisconsin had become quite busy with business and leisure travel, though it lacked the hotel space to house the number of visitors. The Revere and the Tremont, the two largest hotels at the time, routinely would have to turn away potential customers, as they had no more rooms available. Traveling salesmen would commonly refer to Oshkosh's lack of overnight accommodations, causing the city to lose out on further potential economic advantages, as travelers would stay and spend money in Neenah, Menasha or Appleton.

George Athearn, a local entrepreneur and owner of the Revere House in Oshkosh, along with hotels in Fond du Lac and Ashland, heard these complaints and set out to build a lavish hotel the likes of which Oshkosh had never before seen. Immediately, Waters's services were summoned, and his work commenced on the Athearn Hotel.

Waters designed the monstrous hotel, which opened in 1891, in Romanesque style, and the dark-red pressed-brick edifice with cut stone trim dug out of local quarries dominated the cityscape. The main entrance to the hotel was on Division Street, with the ladies' entrance on High Street. The main floor contained a large foyer with marble floors and an exquisite dining room, called the English Room, which held three hundred people and another smaller dining room adjacent, as well as "one of the finest bars in the state." The English Room is still talked about by older generations today, as its mammoth beams of dark oak and intricately framed grand mirrors witnessed two presidents, countless statesmen and politicians and a myriad of celebrities dine within its walls. The fireplaces, one in almost every room in the building, and also framed with elaborately ornamented oak mantels, still reverberate in the memories of those who saw the hotel for themselves.

Athearn Hotel, circa 1923. Demolished in 1964. *Courtesy of the Oshkosh Public Museum.*

View of Main Street and High Avenue intersection looking toward the Athearn with two streetcars, circa 1910. The building on the far right was the Union National Bank, also built by Waters. *Courtesy of the Winnebago County Historical and Archaeological Society.*

The basement level was not spared the luxury. The barbershop featured oak furnishings, silver-plated trim and marble floors, and the billiard room was known to be the most elegant in the state, surpassing even those in Milwaukee. Each private room contained a fireplace, and the building was wired for electricity, as well as gas, and fitted for steam-generated heat.

The main entrance was adorned with a limestone porch with a balcony above, and the corner facing Division and High Streets showcased a circular tower, adding to the already impressive visual. "It is doubtful," wrote the *Oshkosh Times* about Waters, "if he has ever produced a more magnificent or handsome structure."

Prior to the hotel's construction, in an 1886 meeting among Oshkosh business leaders discussing the viability of such a hotel in Oshkosh, William Waters said, "I have made careful estimates and am convinced that there is not the least doubt that we can build a hotel for $35,000 or $40,000 which will be second to none within the state other than Milwaukee....I am so confident in it that I have agreed to take stock." The Athearn's final cost was closer to $125,000 in 1891, over $3,000,000 today.

The Athearn was an immediate success. A 40-room addition was built by Waters in 1909, making the 135-room hotel the largest in the state outside of Milwaukee. Oshkosh's initial goal of building a hotel suitable to the city's standing as the state's second-largest city and a center for business and industry was not only met, but largely surpassed. For sixty years, it was the signature building in a city suddenly wrought with signature buildings, most of them designed by the same man.

George Athearn died in the hotel in 1897 after a long illness, though his family continued to own the building until 1944, when it began several changes of hand. By the mid-1950s, however, the Athearn seemed like a castle past its prime. The habits, wants and needs of the typical American traveler while on the road changed. Highways took the potential customer away from local downtown districts, and cheaper, more convenient roadside motels dotted the landscape everywhere, eliminating a large contingent of the Athearn's targeted consumer. In an attempt to recoup some of the loss, the Athearn began to house students of the University of Wisconsin–Oshkosh, which had outgrown its available housing capacity. The once grand hotel had been transformed into a college dorm.

A 1924 postcard of an artist's rendering of the Athearn Hotel. *Courtesy of the Oshkosh Public Library.*

By the early 1960s, the Athearn was used as permanent housing for elderly residents, similar to the fate of another Waters's work in its waning years three decades later, the Menasha Hotel. By then, building codes had evolved. Much of how the hotel was built would need renovation to pass current inspections, and the costs of such were simply not feasible for such an establishment long past its heyday. Ironically, a cut corner in its construction may have been the final nail in the Athearn's coffin. To keep costs down, the Athearn was framed with wood and overlaid with brick when originally erected in 1891. The building would've needed to be entirely reframed with steel to pass building inspections of the 1960s.

In 1964, the building was sold to the New American Bank of Oshkosh, which wasn't about to pay for such an overhaul. The forty-eight permanent residents of the hotel were given about thirty days to vacate, one of the last being Dolly Athearn, George Athearn's daughter-in-law, who lived in the hotel for fifty years. Demolition came the following month.

The Grand Opera House as it originally appeared, 1887. After falling into disrepair in the 1960s and '70s, and nearly being razed, the building was saved and beautifully restored. *Courtesy of the Oshkosh Public Library.*

Across the way from the Athearn was another William Waters jewel, the Grand Opera House, which opened eight years prior to the hotel, making for one of the Fox Valley's poshest intersections at the turn of the century. Oshkosh had several prior opera houses, though one burned in 1874 and another was destroyed by the flames of the Great Fire of 1875. A third was built, but apparently the residents were unimpressed, as they demonstrated demand for another and Waters didn't disappoint.

Opening in 1883, the Grand was touted as one of the finest opera houses in the west. Situated on High Street, the imposing building was constructed of brick on a stone foundation with bands of black worked in to break up the solid, cream-colored brick walls. The front of the building featured large wooden triple doors above concrete steps leading from the sidewalk, extending the entire twenty-foot length of the main entrance, above which was an intricate balcony lighted by four gas lamps.

Inside the main entrance, a large, high-ceilinged foyer welcomed the visitor. Sitting rooms on either side were equipped with fireplaces framed

Commercial National Bank on College Avenue and Oneida Street in Appleton. Built by Waters in 1881, it was purchased by Irving Zuelke in 1926. It burned to the ground in 1928. The Zuelke Building stands there now. *Courtesy of the Appleton Public Library.*

George A. Whiting residence. Built by Waters in 1897, it was razed by Whiting's grandson George Whiting II in 1957. *Courtesy of the Neenah Historical Society.*

with beautiful solid-wood mantels for the women to warm themselves before taking their seats, which were beyond heavy, elegant drapery separating the entrance hall from the auditorium. The auditorium ceiling featured rich, dark-wood crossbeams resting on massive turned columns rising up on either side of the stage, which was in full view from any given seat in the theater, fitting in almost 1,200 people at full capacity. Warm hues of maroon and olive green accented with gold stenciling colored the ceiling between the beams, with a large center panel featuring a blue sky, clouds and numerous cherubs representing various aspects of mother nature. Above the stage on a ceiling panel was a portrait of William Shakespeare with female muses on either side holding wreaths in homage to the greatest dramatist of all. Supported by columns of copper bronze, the balcony rose in the back of the auditorium. Shades of Pompeiian red with gold accenting covered the wooden railings in front of the first row of seats.

The opera house was a pillar of opulence in its day and hosted many national touring celebrities and stage shows, attended by much of the Fox Valley's elite. Will Rogers, Helen Keller, Houdini, the Barrymores and the

Marx Brothers are some names that graced the stage, many of whom then stayed at the Athearn Hotel.

As was the case with countless other venues meant for the stage, however, the Grand struggled with the rapid popularity of film and the silver screen. By mid-century, it was beginning a long, downward spiral. It was sold and resold and converted to a movie theater. The wooden triple doors of the main entrance were boarded shut, and a smaller, much less impressive entrance was cut into the southeast corner of the building, above which was put a modern marquee. The Grand changed its name, was converted to an adult-movie theater and finally closed in the early 1980s. What was once one of the finest street corners in the Fox Valley had lost its landmark Athearn Hotel in the 1960s and was on the verge of losing its Grand Opera House two decades later. "You wouldn't call it 'grand' now unless you viewed it through the eyes of memory," stated the *Northwestern* in 1981.

A 1981 referendum in Oshkosh asking residents if the city should purchase and restore the building passed fairly easily. However, virtually everything inside the building, with the exception of the balcony, had been lost to the passage of time and decades of renovations. The entire interior had to be painstakingly re-created, literally from the ground up.

The Grand remains standing in Oshkosh today, a testament to its citizens who chose to keep a remnant of the city's past glory rather than surrender it to the wrecking ball. Although the building survives, its history as a destination site for Fox Cities high society has long since faded away. The building, which at one time was a cultural icon in a city beaming with industry and commerce, retains its visual prominence in today's modern city as it sits across from a city block containing a nondescript recent bank building and parking lot. It was on this block that a hotel once stood, the only hotel for miles suitable to accommodate the famous acts performing across the street at the Grand Opera House.

RICH MAN, POOR MAN; GONE JUST THE SAME

There was a wide discrepancy between the haves and the have-nots in the Fox Cities in the latter part of the nineteenth century, as well as after the next century's turn. The rich lived in palatial mansions, built by the finest architects, with interior features of the highest quality. Their employees, suffice to say, did not. Mill owners literally built boardinghouses, neighborhoods and entire towns for their employees, all in the name of keeping the product line moving along.

What was good for the company, however, was usually good for the employee. The practice of societal building created long-standing security for the company as well as for the employees and their families, along with a commonality among people that led to the forming of neighborhood associations and tight-knit communities spanning generations, even lasting to this present day.

The Village of Kimberly, referenced earlier, was created for the specific purpose of housing workers for Kimberly-Clark's mammoth paper mill built there in 1889, the namesake of the village also being the company's cofounder, John Alfred Kimberly. In a 1906 article, the *Post-Crescent* had an interesting take on the Village of Kimberly:

> *Somewhere over in Europe, when knighthood was in flower, there was a little village built around a castle, a big building of stone.*
>
> *A rich knight owned the castle and the cottages of the villagers and the people worked for him. In return they got food and clothes and shelter. They were dependent upon the knight in the castle.*

Road builders in Neenah, circa 1910. *Courtesy of the Neenah Public Library.*

> *If he chose to leave the castle and go to another part of the country and build another village around his castle he could do so. But it would kill the village.*
>
> *On the Fox River, about four miles from Appleton, is a little village built around a big structure of stone, a monster paper mill, more wonderful than any feudal castle.*
>
> *A rich company owns the mill and the houses in which the villagers live. The villagers work for the owners of the big stone and brick building and in return they get food and clothes and shelter…*
>
> *Kimberly is built around the big Kimberly and Clark company's paper mill. The mill is the life of the village, its reason for existence and the village is as dependent upon the mill for life as animals are upon air.*

Kimberly-Clark built about sixty houses to rent to employees and their families, as well as a boardinghouse called the Kimberly Hotel, which housed mostly single males, two to a room, as each worked a different shift at the mill. Soon, employees began purchasing their own lots in Kimberly and building their own houses. After a short while, a school was built, and then a butcher shop, church, general stores and a saloon. By 1905, the

Employees pose in the Kimberly Mill bowling alley, circa 1910. *Courtesy of the Kimberly Public Library.*

Kimberly Hotel after the fire of 1913. The hotel would be rebuilt, though mystery surrounds its fate. *Courtesy of the Kimberly Public Library.*

The Paine Row houses as they appear today, a living example of early twentieth-century employer boardinghouses. *Courtesy of the Scott Wittman Visual, 2018.*

View of mansions along Neenah's Wisconsin Avenue. *Courtesy of the Neenah Historical Society.*

The first C.B. Clark home, built in 1873, and George O. Bergstrom's home, built in 1894, both by William Waters. Both still stand on Wisconsin Avenue, though the Clark home is unrecognizable. *Courtesy of the Neenah Historical Society.*

Village of Kimberly was a full-on community with a commercial downtown and interurban access, connecting it to Appleton, Kaukauna and the rest of the Fox Valley. The presence of the mill also led to further growth of its neighboring villages, Little Chute and Combined Locks.

Opening in 1890 and remodeled in 1909, the Kimberly Hotel was another structure built by the Kimberly-Clark company utilizing the designs of William Waters. A fire severely damaged the building in the winter of 1913, taking out the entire third floor and much else. The hotel was rebuilt by Waters and opened later that same year. The story of the hotel's life span remains a bit of a mystery, as accounts after the fire of 1913 are sparse, except for mundane business meetings in its dining hall and another fire in 1926, though apparently not serious. The building, which used to stand near the present corner of Main Street and Maes Avenue, somewhat disappears from the record.

J.A. Kimberly himself, however, was living quite well in an opulent neighborhood on East Wisconsin Avenue in Neenah, dubbed "Millionaire's Row." Mere feet from where the current Legacy Park now stands, paying homage to the paper pioneers of the Fox Cities with the salvaged remains of a demolished mill, a stretch of the same road reaching toward Lake Winnebago is lined with the former mansions of the nineteenth-century barons. It was here, in these very yards, that the Kimberlys, Clarks, Babcocks, Shattucks, Bergstroms, Sherrys and more spent their leisure time at home, entertained and raised their children. Many of the mansions remain, still glistening in their grandeur as they were when they were built, many by William Waters between the 1870s and 1920s. Walking in the neighborhood today, one may be inclined to believe he or she has been transported into *The Great Gatsby*, as one stately mansion after another appears behind professionally groomed landscaping bordering the blue waters of the largest lake in the state not named Michigan or Superior.

One of these mansions belonged to John Stevens, a leader and financier in local flour mills and inventor of milling machinery and techniques for flouring. Stevens, after patenting his numerous inventions, sold the usage

The John Stevens home on Wisconsin Avenue in Neenah, circa 1904. Built in 1885, it was abandoned by the 1930s and razed in the 1940s. *Courtesy of the Neenah Historical Society.*

John Stevens's boat *Cambria* docked in Riverside Park. *Courtesy of the Neenah Historical Society.*

rights to flour mills in Minneapolis, creating a new behemoth flouring industry in Minnesota, birthing the rise of Pillsbury and General Mills, though virtually killing the industry in Neenah, biting the hand that fed him. The coming of the paper mills, however, many of which began in converted flour mills, made everyone forget about that, and Stevens retired a millionaire at forty years old.

As most Fox Cities millionaires in 1885 who were looking to build a home did, Stevens commissioned William Waters for his massive Queen Anne–style mansion on Wisconsin Avenue. Here, Stevens would dock his yacht, *Cambria*, on which he often pleasure-cruised for most of his remaining life. An account from an 1897 *Post-Crescent* piece details the once commonplace excursions featuring the area's royalty of yesteryear:

> *The steam yacht,* Cambria, *Col. Stevens in command, left this morning for a pleasure trip up the Wolf River. The party on board consisted of Col. And Mrs. John Stevens and son Schuyler, Mr. and Mrs. John Stevens Jr. of Appleton, Fred Rickerson of Milwaukee, Col. And Mrs. George A. Whiting, Mr. and Mrs. Havilah Babcock, Mr. and Mrs. J.A. Kimberly, and Charles R. Smith, of Neenah. The party numbered about*

15 and will be gone several days, stopping en route at Gills Landing where they will make a trip on the Central Line up to Whiting and look over the mammoth paper mills, returning and continuing up the river to New London.

Stevens died in Neenah in 1920 at age seventy-nine. Years later, the mansion was unoccupied and virtually abandoned. In 1937, teenagers, who were apparently entering the mansion for the better part of a year, used it as a "shooting gallery," blasting bullets through the walls, ceilings and windows and tearing up the floors. Later that year, the Neenah Yacht Club purchased the home to utilize as its clubhouse and began restorations. The club's time in the home was short-lived, and the wrecking ball came in 1940, leaving the basement, complete with a bowling alley, exposed for some time after.

The homes of brothers D.W. and George O. Bergstrom also both displayed the lavish fruits of their life's labor. George built his home on Wisconsin Avenue in 1894 among the other glorious mansions of the day, though D.W. built his on the west side of town a year earlier, on the corner of Church and Sherry Streets. Although the brothers were business partners in the Bergstrom Stove Factory, their wives did not get along and apparently were not even on speaking terms, so the brothers elected to build away from each

D.W. Bergstrom home. Its razing in 1965 for a post office renewed efforts in Neenah for local historic preservation. *Courtesy of the Neenah Public Library.*

other to avoid any potential conflicts. William Waters designed a Queen Anne–style home for George, with an exterior of wood shingles, clapboard and limestone and featuring two circular towers.

D.W. also had Waters build him a Queen Anne, though his home was the larger, more visually striking of the two—especially the interior. Just inside the front door was a large foyer featuring oak walls lined with gold-embossed trim reflecting light from a highly polished brass and glass chandelier, welcoming the many visitors to the home. The living room showcased a massive cherrywood fireplace and opened into the smaller of two libraries in the home, with countless books lining mahogany shelves. Dark, rich woods ran throughout the home, accented by oriental rugs in deep red hues and large windows allowing in abundant natural light.

After George Bergstrom bought out his brother for sole ownership of the stove factory in 1904, he sold his home several years later, living and ultimately dying in the hotel designed by his son, the Valley Inn. His home still stands on Wisconsin Avenue.

Twelve hours after the death of his younger brother, D.W. Bergstrom passed away in his home at age eighty. The fate of his opulent home was not as fortunate as that of his brother's. His daughter continued to live in the home for many years after his death, though inexplicably, the City of Neenah had the house razed in 1965 to build a new post office on the site, "which, in 75 or 100 years," according to the *Oshkosh Northwestern*, "may be itself razed to make way for still another structure marking the progress of time." Although the post office still stands in operation, the razing of the D.W. Bergstrom home is often cited today as sparking renewed interest and vigor in historic preservation efforts in Neenah.

Oshkosh also had its posh neighborhoods for wealthy lumber kings and business elite. Most of the prominent industry leaders, such as Philetus Sawyer and his son, Edgar P. Sawyer, built their homes north of the Fox River on Algoma Boulevard.

Born, coincidentally, in Whiting, Vermont, and raised in New York, Philetus Sawyer found his way to Oshkosh after all the timber was harvested back east, where he was working in the sawmills. By 1853, he was the owner of a sawmill in Oshkosh and purchased huge swaths of lush forests in the north, and he was soon enjoying self-made affluence as a lumberman. Beloved in Oshkosh by all classes, Sawyer went on to become mayor, a state representative, a five-term elected member of the U.S. House of Representatives and finally a two-term U.S. senator, serving until 1893.

Home of Senator Philetus Sawyer, circa 1887. Purchased by the Paine Lumber Company and eventually razed in 1936. Now the site of Hiker Park, Oshkosh. *Courtesy of the Oshkosh Public Library.*

Edgar P. Sawyer home, built in 1872. Sawyer himself had the home razed to build a larger one, which is now the Oshkosh Public Museum. *Courtesy of the Winnebago County Historical and Archaeological Society.*

Sawyer showcased his wealth by erecting a grand Italianate mansion on the corner of Algoma Boulevard and West Algoma Boulevard (Congress Avenue today). The mansion's exterior featured pedimented windows, sophisticated cornice work, a large, angled triple bay window on the second floor and a massive intricately detailed balustrade veranda covering three quarters of the home above an elegantly columned front porch. The entire front yard of the home, which was the scene of many weddings and social events in Oshkosh high society, was groomed as a formal flower garden with buckthorn bushes throughout.

After Sawyer's death in 1900, the 1857 home was passed along to his granddaughter, who sold it several years later to the Paine Lumber Company. The house sat empty and abandoned for several years, and Paine later sold it to a salvage company. The Philetus Sawyer home, which stood where Hiker Park is today, was demolished in 1936, with little information left as to why.

Philetus's son, Edgar, watched over his father's business holdings while his father was performing his civic duties, eventually becoming a business partner in P. Sawyer and Son, which was producing five million board feet of lumber a year.

In 1872, Edgar Sawyer built his home across Congress Avenue from his father's and spared no expense. Edgar built a mammoth high-style Second Empire home with an imposing central tower, corniced eaves, and intricate ornamental detail. The home and grounds covered an entire block surrounded by an iron gate with front stone pillars. Edgar, however, apparently became bored with the home, as he had the entire house knocked down to build an even bigger one on the same site. In 1908, William Waters built the new home, which Sawyer spent little time in after the death of his wife just a year later. In 1922, Edgar Sawyer donated the home to the City of Oshkosh, where it still stands proud today as the Oshkosh Public Museum.

Built in the same neighborhood, about three years after Philetus Sawyer's home was erected, was the home of Edward L. Paine, founder of Paine Lumber Company. The large pre–Civil War, wood-frame mansion featured a corner tower cupola with double-arched windows on all four sides, rising over the landscape. Gabled roofs with elegantly detailed ornamentation under the peaks adjoined abundant windows, allowing the most sunlight possible to stream through, which was undoubtedly hazed with sawdust at times. It was in this home that Edward's successors as president of Paine Lumber grew up—sons Charles and George.

Edward L. Paine residence in Oshkosh. Built by the lumber tycoon in 1860 and razed in 1955. *Courtesy of the Paine Art Center and Gardens.*

The Nathan Paine mansion, now the Paine Art Center and Gardens in Oshkosh. Construction began in 1925, though the Paines never lived in the home. *Courtesy of the Paine Art Center and Gardens.*

After Edward's death in 1893, his grandsons, Edward W. and Nathan, who would both also follow in the family business—Nathan ascending to company president after the death of his father, George, in 1917—lived in the home. In April 1896, an evening remembered for generations occurred as Nathan Paine married Jessica Kimberly, the daughter of John Alfred Kimberly, at the Kimberly mansion on Wisconsin Avenue in Neenah.

In 1927, Nathan began construction on a mammoth Tudor Revival estate across Algoma Boulevard from where the Philetus Sawyer home stood. The lavish, sprawling mansion would exude the opulence of the once dominant lumber kings, as the home featured an interior of rich oak and walnut and lush polished limestone, and showcased a bountiful collection of fine furnishings and visual arts. Vast gardens and an arboretum spread throughout the landscape, inspired by Nathan and Jessica's love for their English countryside heritage.

Nathan and Jessica Paine, however, never lived in the mansion. The Depression hit Nathan's interests hard, and all construction was suspended in 1932. After years of little activity at the home, it was established in 1948 as an art museum, which it remains as today, serving as a stark reminder of fortunes gained and lost in the remnants of "Sawdust City."

In 1954, as the Paine Art Center planned to expand the arboretum, an old house adjacent to the grounds needed to be removed to complete the desired result. In January of the following year, down came the ninety-five-year-old home of Colonel Edward L. Paine.

Richard T. Morgan's home was another landmark from the affluent lumber days that did not survive into present times. The mansion, at 214 Jackson Street, was razed in 1938 after sitting abandoned for a number of years. Built around 1868 by the cofounder of Morgan Brothers Lumber Company, the home sat empty after it was last occupied by Morgan's daughter after his death.

The *Northwestern* reported on the razing:

> *The old house, elegant in its furnishings, was the scene of many brilliant social activities. For a number of years, following Mr. Morgan's death, it was occupied by his daughter, Mrs. Gilbert Drew. They were the last occupants of the house which has stood vacant for nearly a score of years.*
>
> *Workmen razing the house today found copies of the* Oshkosh Northwestern *dated 1895, stuffed beneath the carpeting in the playroom. They counted 159 doors, all made of solid lumber.*

Richard T. Morgan's home, circa 1887. The home at 214 Jackson Street was razed in 1938. *Courtesy of the Oshkosh Public Library.*

The home of Richard's brother and lumber company co-founder, John R. Morgan, still stands and is the current home of the Winnebago County Historical & Archaeological Society, lavishly restored to its originally intended appearance.

High above the Fox, where the river used to pour itself over a rocky ledge and into raging rapids as it continued its 170-foot drop, rise tall bluffs overlooking a vast scene of winding waters and abundant greenery. Upon this bluff, along what is today West Prospect Avenue, is where the affluent of Appleton built their homes in the latter part of the nineteenth century and into the twentieth, after the river had been dammed and locked for passage and harnessed for power. The neighborhood showcased a myriad of architectural styles, including Italianate, Colonial Revival, Tudor and Renaissance Revival, among others, built and lived in by names familiar to Appleton's history, such as Erb, Conkey, Boldt and Bertschy.

Gabled roofs, columned front porches, pedimented doors and windows, stucco finishes and three-story towers lived in harmony with each other along the prominent bluff-side street. Two shining examples of Italian Villa architecture designed by William Waters were erected on the street as well, both still standing but somewhat lost amongst the shuffle of a thriving, twenty-first-century city that had barely eight thousand residents when the majority of the neighborhood was built.

The fact that the bluff overlooked an unmatched view of the city was not the only reason the site was desired by homeowners. The location also overlooked the mills along the river below, mills that those erecting the houses were responsible for. The grand H.J. Rogers mansion, another

City Park neighborhood in Appleton appearing much like it did at the turn of the twentieth century. The home in the back right with the double row of windows was the Ferber residence. *Courtesy of Scott Wittman Visual, 2018.*

Temple Zion. Built by Harry Houdini's father, Rabbi Mayer Samuel Weiss. The family left Appleton before the temple opened. *Courtesy of Scott Wittman Visual, 2018.*

D.L. Libbey home. Utilized for a time by the State Normal School and razed in 1928. *Courtesy of the Winnebago County Historical and Archaeological Society.*

Waters masterpiece, and the home of John Van Nortwick also were built on the bluff, watching over their Appleton Pulp and Paper Mill below.

Sadly, the Van Nortwick home was demolished sometime before 1935, along with many other pioneering homes throughout the years in the "Old Third Ward." The community has been a constant site of growth in the name of progress over the last 140 years, as its central location in Appleton has led to the demise of many homes and buildings as newer, more modern structures have been erected. Located just two blocks from College Avenue, the Old Third Ward neighborhood has been disrupted for generations, as city and county facilities have spread throughout the area and continue to sprawl. For the homes that remain, many carriage houses have been wiped away for modern garages, and alterations have subdued the once abundant grandeur of the old neighborhood.

After about 1910, the lots on the bluff were taken up, and potential home builders looked northeast of the College Avenue commercial district and close to Lawrence University, where another neighborhood popular with the commercial elite was building up surrounding City Park. Although the homes and lots were smaller than on West Prospect, the houses were among the finest examples of various architectural styles in the state. Queen Anne, Arts and Crafts, Craftsman and period revival homes interspersed with Neo-Gothic churches, creating an eclectic and visually unique community. It was in this neighborhood that a young Edna Ferber lived and wrote, and Rabbi Samuel Weiss, the father of Harry Houdini, had the Temple Zion built, though the rabbi left the city before the temple was ready for service.

As the community was in such proximity to Lawrence University, as the school expanded, the number of historically significant homes contracted. A multitude of homes in central Appleton have been demolished over the decades for the growth and expansion of the college. Homes, including those designed by architects Waters and Hove, have been razed to make way for the Worcester Art Center, Downer Commons, Kohler Hall, the Music-Drama Center, along with a myriad of others.

Lawrence University is not alone in its history of demolition practices for the expansion of educational campuses in the Fox Valley. The University of Wisconsin–Oshkosh has its own list of conquests, dating back to when it was called the Oshkosh State Normal School. As the university grew along Algoma Boulevard, former mansions of the city's past affluence were swept up in the progress, some being incorporated into the campus, some swept away entirely.

One of these was the home of Daniel L. Libbey, at one time one of the most prominent employers in all of Oshkosh. Libbey was president of numerous companies, including the Oshkosh Carriage Company, Williamson & Libbey Lumber Company and the Oshkosh Water Works Company, supporting thousands of employees and their families. "There has never been an enterprise which pointed to the good of the city that Mr. Libbey has not aided with his money and his influence," claimed the *Northwestern* in 1884.

Libbey's former home on Algoma Boulevard was purchased by the school after his death and utilized as a science hall in the 1920s. After a new science building was constructed around 1928, the home was razed to make room for further expansion, and more historic homes would meet the same fate.

EPILOGUE

The challenge of balancing progress and preservation has been a societal struggle for generations, and likely will continue to be so. Unfortunately, there remains no easy formula for determining when and if razing a historic property is necessary to obtain progress, and if the options must be mutually exclusive.

What does remain necessary, however, is continuing to tell the stories of our past even when the physical structures have been long wiped from the landscape. The stories of the people who built those structures, the people who lived in them, worked in them, sacrificed for them.

The Fox Cities area was transformed from a frontier wilderness to a sprawling industrious community in less than one average human life span. Today's residents are comprised of the descendants of those who made that community: the mill workers, the loggers, the canal builders, the dredgers, the lock tenders, the immigrants, the tycoons, the financiers, the barons.

As a historical researcher, one thing I am always struck by is the myriad of stories in old newspapers detailing the plights and the sacrifices of those before us. These were the days before workplace regulations, before the EPA, before OSHA, before every person seemingly had some kind of a safety net protecting him or her from anything and everything. Their stories need to be told as well. Their sacrifices should be known and honored.

There is no historical sign placed at the site where twelve-year-old Theresa Cindel was run over by a train outside the Atlas Mill in 1888 as she brought her father, who was employed there, his dinner. There is no plaque anywhere detailing the 1904 death of Dominick Munette, or the 1888 death of Fred Hedky; both were employees at Kaukauna paper mills, both were wrapped around line shafts, their bodies literally torn to pieces. None either for George Reyba, crushed by machinery at Thilmany in 1932, or for Joseph Monday in 1904 and Joseph Esdepskyim 1901—both were painters who plunged to their deaths off scaffolding—or for Charles De Young, lock tender at Lock No. 4 by Interlake Pulp and Paper Mill, who was struck by a rebounding turn crank and drowned in the tailrace of the mill. Old newspapers are littered with such accounts virtually daily.

It is not a physical building that would hold their memory. It is only the researcher who can do that. The preserver of our history is not in limestone and brick, but only in accounts of everyday life. Perhaps it is not the physical that holds our history, but rather our own self-initiated awareness of who we are.

The following is a poem printed in the September 20, 1875 *Oshkosh Northwestern*, soon after the great fire of that same year that leveled the city. It was buried in a 143-year-old newspaper, of which, if not for my research for this book, I would have likely remained unfamiliar. As saving every building is an unwinnable battle, perhaps this is where our efforts should lie:

It was on a spring-time sunset, close upon that dreadful day,
When our Oshkosh in the ashes of her desolation lay.
That I wandered through the ruins, o'er the fragments black and bare–
Sole mementoes left, alas! Of long, long years of toil and care!
Oh! The sight was soul depressing; structures, gardens, trees, and flowers,
Leveled into smoking cinders in those few but frantic hours!
Stately piles and modest homes which stood attesting skill and taste
Were destroyed, and in their place there lay a devastated waste!
Onward strolled I, sad and thoughtful, past the fallen tow'rs and domes-
Past the crowds of relic-seekers on the sites of wealthy homes.
Past the court house standing witness of a brave deed nobly done–
Onward where the Winnebago sparkled in the sinking sun.
The dreary streets behind me stretched their ashen lengths along–
Far behind me was the curious and sensation-seeking throng.
On my right and left was silence–yes a silence like to death!
Save myself there was no creature there which drew a living breath!
Sore oppressed I sought a resting-place against a ruined wall
And listened to the whisper of the waters rise and fall,
Till I heard a hasty footstep and, half-startled turned to see

If another mournful meditator shared the scene with me.
And I saw a woman worn and wan, with pallid haggard face,
And clad in rusty mourning robes, come quickly to the place;
With anxious penetrating glances searched she left and right,
No single timber, stick nor stone escaped her eager sight!
In motionless astonishment I stood half hidden by
A giant tree, whose burned and leafless arms reached wide and high,
And watched her narrowly, as now and then unto the ground
She stooped, and gazed intently at some remnant she had found;
While ever and anon she turned the smoking rubbish o'er
And still searched on untiringly as she had done before.
At length from out the ruins, after long and patient toil,
She drew a tiny casket tarnished both by fire and soil;
With an eager eye she pressed it to her lips and to her heart,
Then seized a stone and deftly dashed the binding clasps apart.
Instinctively I nearer drew, that I might also see
The rare and valued treasure which I therein enclosed might be:
Though she saw me then, she gave no indication of surprise,
She offered no resistance as I bent to view the prize,
And so I saw–what think you was the treasure lying there?
The charred but perfect out-lines of a baby's curl of hair!
It was but one fleeting moment that we gazed upon its form,
In the tarnished, battered casket from its fire-ordeal yet warm;
As the cold lake breeze of ev'ning, gently breathed along the shore
The little ringlet quivered first, then vanished evermore!
Then as if by strong hand smitten, sunk that poor, wan woman down.
With her haggard feature hidden in her shabby morning gown,
And she moaned as there she lay amid the cinders, dust and dew,
"O, my baby! O, my baby! It was all was all was left of you!"
Then I spoke; "My friend, look up, and let me help you rise, I pray!
O, surely this will injure you! O, do not so give way!"
She heeded not, nor answered me, she only sobbed anew,
"My baby, O, my baby! It was all was left of you!"
"But your baby is in heaven–you will find him there at last,
And the bliss of the reunion, shall requite the painful past-"
Still she moaned with countenance yet hidden from my anxious view,
"O, my baby! O, my baby! It was all was left of you!"
Oh! It seemed so coldly cruel to forsake her in her grief,
And I tried by speech and action to suggest some slight relief;

"Friend," I said, "I pray you tell me is there naught that I can do?"
Still the same cry, "O, my baby! O, my baby! It was all was left of you."
Then I strove once more to raise her and to speak some helpful word,
But she gave no sign nor motion that could indicate she heard;
Still she sobbed as there I left her prone amid the dust and dew,
"O, my baby! O, my baby! It was all was left of you!"
On that day were tender voices of fond hopes forever hushed–
Fortunes lost and homes demolished and ambitious spirits crushed–
Yet I ween there was no instance of more pitiful despair,
Than that mother's, o'er the ashes of her buried baby's hair!

Sept. 20th, 1875. M.E. Harmon

BIBLIOGRAPHY

Adams, Peter J. "Historical Society Brings 9/11 Remembrance Home." *Appleton Post-Crescent*, September 7, 2011.

Alderson, Kate. "Attempts Made to Save Grand." *Oshkosh Northwestern*, February 22, 1980.

Appleton Crescent. "Is Master of Locks and Bolts." July 23, 1904.

———. "Opening of the New Theatre." February 15, 1902.

Appleton Evening Crescent. "Commercial Club Plan." January 3, 1903.

———. "Kimberly-Clark to Help Appleton." January 4, 1910.

———. "Roberts' Resort." June 5, 1897.

———. "The Steamer *Evelyn* Has Been Condemned." June 29, 1907.

———. "Was Not So Warm." April 30, 1902.

Appleton Post. "The Atlas Gone; Fire Again Visits Our Water Power." June 14, 1888.

———. "Paper Making Center of the West." November 16, 1882.

———. "The Wall Paper Industry." October 23, 1892.

Appleton Post Annual Review. "The Young Idea." December 21, 1882.

Appleton Post-Crescent. "Canals Made Fox River Useful as Water Highway." May 28, 1948.

———. "Draws History of Industry in Valley Region." October 1, 1932.

———. "Flour Mills Preceded Paper Mills Here." May 28, 1948.

———. "Fox Officials Arrive Here for Theatre Opening." November 15, 1929.

———. "Gilbert Paper Plans $100,000 Plant Addition." July 15, 1959.

———. "Hotel Athearn to be Razed." August 1, 1964.

———. "Kurz Recalls First Days in Light Plant." September 29, 1932.
———. "Lock Master Retires After 39 Years of Service." August 23, 1930.
———. "Mike Kirby Died Today." February 24, 1911.
———. "Once-Famous Neenah Summer Resort to Suffer Inevitable Fate of Progress." August 1, 1965.
———. "One of World's Greatest Industries, Result of Fifty Years of Effort." January 4, 1923.
———. "Rio Theater to Close Doors." June 20, 1959.
———. "Where History Repeats Itself." February 22, 1906.
Associated Press. "Gilbert Mill to Close Mill in Menasha in November." October 4, 2001.
Behnke, Duke. "Neenah Clock Tower Restoration Project Takes First Step." *Appleton Post-Crescent*, September 24, 2008.
Bernstein, Mark, and William Hoest. *Paper with Presence: A Gilbert Century.* Menasha, WI: Gilbert Paper, 1987.
Boardman, Arlen. "The Life and Legend of the Consolidated Mill." *Appleton Post-Crescent*, September 19, 1982.
Bollier, Jeff. "Slow Going." *Oshkosh Northwestern*, November 8, 2009.
Bremer, William W., and Holly J. Lyon. *"A Little Ways Ahead": The Centennial History of Thilmany Pulp & Paper Company Kaukauna, Wisconsin.* Kaukauna, WI: Thilmany Pulp & Paper Company, a Division of Hammermill Paper Company, 1983.
Brooker, David. "Edison's Filament Had Hardly Cooled When Appleton Had Electric Lights." *Appleton Post-Crescent*, October 19, 1954.
Brooker, Tom. "K-C Begins Razing of old Main Office." *Appleton Post-Crescent*, February 27. 1980.
Chambers, Tom. "Fire! Fire at Morgans!" *Prairie, Pines, and People; Winnebago County in a New Perspective*, edited by James I. Metz. Oshkosh, WI: Oshkosh Northwestern Company, 1976.
Church, Frank. "Economics Forced Barges Off the River." *Appleton Post-Crescent*, July 3, 1981.
———. "Thrills, Romance in Those Riverboats." *Appleton Post-Crescent*, July 2, 1981.
Crane, Virginia Glenn. *The Oshkosh Woodworkers' Strike of 1898: A Wisconsin Community in Crisis.* Self-published, 1998.
Cunningham, G.A. *History of Neenah.* Neenah, WI: Neenah Gazette, 1878.
Ekvall, Allan. "One Month Left for Old Oshkosh Hotel." *Appleton Post-Crescent*, August 2, 1964.

Federal Writers' Project of the Works Progress Administration. *The WPA Guide to Wisconsin: The Federal Writers' Project Guide to 1930s Wisconsin.* Introduction by Norman K. Risjord. St. Paul: Minnesota Historical Society Press, 2006

Ferber, Edna. *A Peculiar Treasure.* New York: Literary Guild of America, 1939

Fitzgerald, Sean. "Old Factory Coming Down." *Oshkosh Northwestern,* December 12, 2001.

Fries, Robert F. *Empire in Pine: The Story of Lumbering in Wisconsin 1830–1900.* Madison: State Historical Society of Wisconsin, 1951.

Gard, Robert E., and Elaine Reetz. *The Trail of the Serpent: The Fox River Valley Lore and Legend.* Madison: Wisconsin House Ltd., 1973.

Glaab, Charles N., and Lawrence H. Larsen. *Factories in the Valley.* Madison: State Historical Society of Wisconsin, 1969.

Grey, Dave. "Paine Lumber Property Taking Shape as River Mill." *Oshkosh Northwestern,* January 4, 1987.

Groth, David, and Patti Pata. *A Compilation of Articles Pertaining to the Works of Architect William Waters.* Oshkosh, WI: Winnebago County Historical and Archaeological Society, 2000.

Hall, Sylvia. *Farewell to the Homeland: European Immigration to N.E. Wisconsin 1840–1900.* Green Bay, WI: Brown County Historical Society, 1984.

Hinant, Mike. "State Archaeologist to Dig for Site." *Appleton Post-Crescent,* June 14, 1978.

Jungwirth, Clarence J. *A History of Oshkosh The Early Years, Vol.1.* Self-published, 1993.

———. *A History of the Bloody Sixth Ward in the City of Oshkosh 1880–1940.* Self-published, 1991.

Karstaedt, Clinton F. *Oshkosh 100 Years a City 1853–1953.* Oshkosh, WI: Castle-Pierce Printing Company, 1953.

Kimberly-Clark. *Four Men and a Machine: Commemorating the Seventy-Fifth Anniversary of Kimberly-Clark Corporation.* Neenah, WI: 1947.

Kinzie, Juliette, A. *Wau-Bun: The Early Day in the Northwest.* Cincinnati: Derby and Jackson, 1856.

Koene, Mary Ann. "Regrets Too Late for Athearn." *Oshkosh Northwestern,* December 16, 1984.

———. "Wood Construction Doomed Hotel." *Oshkosh Northwestern,* December 16, 1984.

Kort, Ellen. *The Fox Heritage: A History of Wisconsin's Fox River Valley.* Woodland Hills, CA: Windsor Publications, 1984.

Mackesy, Lillian. "Appleton's 'Opera House.'" *Appleton Post-Crescent,* May 3, 1970.

———. "Oshkosh Man Fell in Love with Fox River and Its Steamboats." *Appleton Post-Crescent,* August 28, 1966.

Metz, James I. *Oshkosh Aflame!: Traumas and Triumphs of its Sawdust Citizens (A History)*. Oshkosh, WI: Polemics Press, 1999.

Meyer, James. "Link to Past." *Appleton Post-Crescent*, February 10, 1997.

Miller, Cliff. "Workers Worried but Still See Mill Shutdown Delay." *Appleton Post-Crescent*, February 13, 1972.

Mitchell, D.C. *Steamboats on the Fox River: A Pictorial History of Navigation in Northeastern Wisconsin*. Oshkosh, WI: Castle-Pierce Press, 1986.

Morgan, John. "Cook and Brown Decides to Halt Coal Barge Traffic on Fox River." *Appleton Post-Crescent*, August 29, 1960.

Nebel, Richard. William O. *Waters Oshkosh Architect.* http://williamwatersoshkosharchitect.blogspot.com. 2010–2018.

Nickeson, Sandra. "Project Calls for Patience, Volunteers." *Oshkosh Northwestern*, May 22, 1981.

Oberg, Michael Leroy. *Professional Indian: The American Odyssey of Eleazer Williams*. Philadelphia: University of Pennsylvania Press, 2015.

Oshkosh Northwestern. "After the Fire." September 22, 1875.

———. "Another Phoenix City." February 14, 1876.

———. "Architect William Waters Left Imprint on Oshkosh." February 24, 1990.

———. "Atmosphere of Athearn Recalls 'Good Old Days.'" June 19, 1953.

———. "A Dinner Is Booked." September 6, 1916.

———. "Hotel to Be Modern." September 7, 1915.

———. "Memories of River Renewed by Gift." January 26, 1956.

———. "Morgan Company Has Grown Along with City." June 5, 1953.

———. "Old Landmarks at Paine Plant Being Razed." August 29, 1935.

———. "Old Sawyer Home, Landmark Here, Is Being Demolished." March 23, 1936.

———. "Oshkosh. How It Is Viewed by an Outsider." September 20, 1876.

———. "Oshkosh Landmark Being Torn Down." November 17, 1938.

———. "Paine's Oldest Oshkosh Company." June 5, 1953.

———. "Raze Nearly Century-Old Home for Improvement of Arboretum." January 7, 1955.

———. "Say Three Boys Did Damage to Neenah Mansion." February 15, 1937.

———. "Teaming Up with Jeld-Wen Good Strategy." May 8, 2008.

———. "Will Not Run." March 22, 1892.

Peterson, Bernie. "A Piece of Appleton Dies." *Appleton Post-Crescent*, April 8, 1981.

Radin, Paul. *The Winnebago Tribe.* Washington, D.C.: Smithsonian Institution, 1923.

Report of Fox River Locks Task Force. Appleton, WI, 1982.

Roberts, Kay. "An Elegant Resort." *Appleton Post-Crescent*, March 23, 1980.

Rosholt, William. *Pioneers of the Pinery*. Rosholt, WI: Rosholt House, 1979.

Smith, Alice E. *Millstone and Saw: The Origins of Neenah-Menasha*. Madison: State Historical Society of Wisconsin, 1966.

Spector, Robert. *Shared Values: A History of Kimberly-Clark*. Lyme, CT: Greenwich Publishing Group, 1997.

Strange, John G. *Fifty Years of Aspiration: An Abridged History of the Institute of Paper Chemistry.* Appleton, WI: Institute of Paper Chemistry, 1980.

Weber, Jason R. *Kimberly: A Centennial History 1910–2010*. Self-published, 2010.

Wolff, Patricia. "End of Lumber Era." *Oshkosh Northwestern*, June 9, 2009.

Wollangk, JoEllen. *Homestead and Haven: The Charles A. Grignon Mansion*. Appleton, WI: Outagamie County Historical Society Inc., 1998.

INDEX

C

D

E

F

G

S

T

V

W

ABOUT THE AUTHOR

Scott Wittman is a professional historical landscape photographer based in Wisconsin's beautiful Fox River Valley. A native of Appleton, Scott has spent much of his adult life traveling the highways, byways and back roads of this great nation documenting, vis images and words, its people, places and heritage.

A graduate of the Colorado Institute of Art with a degree in photography, Scott has written and created images for a multitude of publications, businesses and online platforms telling the stories of those who have come before and why it's important for future generations to learn from and preserve their memory.

He is the host of the *Trippin' on History* podcast, launching in 2019, and his work can be found at ScottWittmanVisual.com.

Scott lives in Appleton with his wife, Vicky, and three sons—Asa, Jett and Rhodes.